SECRETS
Of The
EARLY
CHURCH

ANDREW STROM

What will it take to get back to the Book of Acts?

RevivalSchool

Secrets of the Early Church

Copyright © 2004-2008 by Andrew Strom

First printing, 2004
Second printing, 2008

Wholesale distribution by Lightning Source, Inc.

ISBN 10: 0-9799073-3-0

ISBN 13: 978-0-9799073-3-3

The Bible Translation primarily used in this book is the New International Version, (c) 1973, 1978 by Bible Society International.

Also used on occasion is the King James Version.

1. Prophets – History   2. Revivals

Table of Contents

1. The Shape of the Church to Come 5

2. The "Nine Lies" 9

3. "Asking Jesus into Your Heart"?? 15

4. Church Buildings 31

5. The "One Man" Pastor System 39

6. "Enforced" Tithing 45

7. Prosperity and "Seed-Faith" 51

8. Is Our "Religious System" Killing People? 59

9. Bible Colleges 65

10. The "Two Secrets" of Revival 71

11. Sunday Disunity 79

12. Now for Love and Simplicity 85

13. Programs and More Programs 91

14. What on Earth is "Koinonia"? 97

15. Last of the Nine – The Gospel of 'Humanism' 107

16. Wrapping it All Up 111

CHAPTER ONE

THE SHAPE OF THE CHURCH TO COME

To start this book, I want you to do something for me. I want you to forget about today's church for a moment – with all her apparent problems and contradictions, and imagine something quite different. I want you to imagine that you are still living in the same city, in the same year, but you are right in the middle of a 'Book of Acts' type scenario. Somehow everything has changed.

For some reason, all of the Spirit-filled Christians in your city have left their Denominations and divisions behind. They have truly begun to fulfill the prayer of Jesus – "That they all may be ONE". They now hold huge gatherings all over the city – right out in the open. And as well as these united gatherings, on most streets there is now a house-meeting, where all the Spirit-filled believers from that street gather together, eating and sharing and having communion, etc. The power of God flowing in these meetings is amazing. Many healings and miracles are happening all over the city

It seems also that the church buildings and cathedrals have simply been abandoned. No longer do Christians want to hide themselves away behind "four walls". They want to gather out where the people are – presenting Jesus to the whole world. They want to be truly "one body". There is no way that any of their old buildings could contain the crowds, anyhow.

And the men whom God has raised up to lead this vast movement do not seem much like the 'Reverends' or even the 'televangelists' of old. In fact, quite a few of them have never been to Bible College and they seem to be very plain, ordinary people from humble backgrounds. But what an anointing! It is very clear to everyone that these 'apostles and prophets' (as they are known) have spent many years in prayer and brokenness before God – drawing closer and closer to Him. When they speak, the very fear of the Lord seems to come down, and many people repent deeply of their sins. Demons are cast out and the blind and crippled are made whole; these kinds of things are happening all the time. The whole city is just in awe of what is going on, and thousands upon thousands are being saved. Even the newspapers and television are full of it.

As soon as someone repents they are immediately baptized in water and hands are laid on them for the infilling of the Holy Spirit – this is expected from day one! And it is also expected that every Christian has a gift and a calling from God – and that they should be encouraged to move forward and fulfill their calling. No longer is there a distinction made between those who are "ministers" and those who are merely 'laity'. Now it is expected that EVERYONE is a minister of the Lord! (However, there are 'elders' – i.e., older Christians to guide things)

Same

Some of the bishops and pastors from several denominations have actually denounced this great move of God very strongly. They say it is "deception" and warn their people to stay away. (Every Revival in history has been accused of this - usually by religious leaders). But to be honest, it is so obvious to most people that God is the One behind it all, that very few take these men seriously. The Spirit of God is sweeping all before Him. The glory of the Lord has come.

One of the reasons that these leaders are so upset is that a lot of the Christians' GIVING now does not go to church buildings, but rather to the POOR. In fact, God has spoken to many people to start supporting widows and orphans overseas, etc. They also give generously to anyone in their midst who is in need. Some even sell their own possessions in order to do this.

The huge over-riding theme of this great movement is LOVE. "Behold how they love one another" is the catch-cry of many who watch this 'new church' in action. And everyone is given to MUCH

PRAYER.

And so, gathering "as one" in the outdoors and breaking bread from house to house, they eat together with glad and sincere hearts, praising God and enjoying the favor of all the people. And the Lord adds to their number daily those who are being saved.

PROVOCATIVE STATEMENTS

The above description is taken straight out of the Book of Acts - as applied to today. Everything in the above paragraphs is put there to give you an idea of what it would be like to live in the Jerusalem church at the start of Acts – and it was like that for YEARS. Imagine the impact of such a church on the world around it! God is wanting to do this again. And He wants to use ordinary people like you and me to help bring it to pass.

I am convinced that we are NOT supposed to treat the early church as a "special case". It was given as an 'example' to us. It is what the "normal" church should be like all the time! And yet we have fallen so far below this standard. Only in times of Revival do we approach it again for a time. But I believe it is supposed to be "normal" for the church to be like this – day in and day out. This is the way that Jesus always wanted us to be.

During the course of this book you will read some very provocative statements – designed to challenge many of the things that we simply take for granted in the church today – for many of these things are not found in the Bible. And I have to ask the question – "Why do we need them then?" Could it be that many of them are just 'traditions' that are actually harming – rather than helping – the church? Isn't it true that we may have to get rid of a bunch of these things to once again live like the Book of Acts?

And so this book is designed to deliberately shock and provoke you into looking at why we do things the way we do. It is designed to make you study and study your Bible to find the answers. It is designed to make you hungry for a different kind of Christianity –

the kind that was actually invented by Jesus and the apostles in the beginning. And this book is also designed to give you some insights into this question – "How exactly do we get back there?" What are the actual STEPS to recovering Book-of-Acts type Christianity again? Not just the outward 'structural' changes but the inward 'heart' changes as well.

As I said, this book is deliberately provocative and challenging. It pulls no punches about the state of our Christianity today. You need to be warned that until you actually go to the Scriptures and study the points I am making, you may be offended by some of the things you read. Many of the things I will be challenging are the 'holy cows' of the way our church is set up today. Are you ready to see them challenged in the light of Scripture?

Hang on to your seats, my friends! Let the 'provocation' begin!

CHAPTER TWO

THE "NINE LIES"

This book first began as a series of articles that I published on our international email List. The series was known as the "Nine Lies of Today's Church." A highly provocative title for a highly provocative series! But the purpose of this series was not just to 'provoke' people. It was also to get them to understand the 'heart-transformation' and the "personal Revival" that we all need to go through if we are to be a part of a Book-of-Acts type church. We need to always keep in mind that along with 'structural' things, there are a lot of 'heart' things that God wants to deal with also

The first article in the series was like an "Introduction" to the entire range of topics that we would be tackling in the series, and thus in a lot of ways it was the most 'provocative' of all. I literally received hundreds upon hundreds of emails about this one article after it was published. In fact, the reaction to it was the largest we had ever seen. When you read it (below), I'm sure you will see why.

THE "NINE LIES" OF TODAY'S CHURCH

It is a sad fact that today's church is deceiving itself in some very crucial areas. Below are some plain facts (absolutely true) that may shock a few people:

1. "Ask Jesus into your heart" is not in the Bible. Neither is "Give your heart to the Lord", or repeating a "Sinner's Prayer". These practices do not exist in Scripture at all. The subject of salvation is the most important subject in the Bible and we are being lied to about it. These doctrines are a total fabrication. They were invented to make salvation "quick and convenient". Many church members today who are relying on these things are clearly not 'saved' at all.

2. _Church buildings do not exist in the Bible._ They were invented [handwritten: ?] around _200-300 AD,_ when the church was in _serious decline._ Only a backslidden church could fall so far away from the simplicity of the early church. Church buildings are _anti-New Testament,_ and bring with them a host of _problems and traditions._ It was basically when the church fell into the _hands of Rome_ that this concept of the _"cathedral"_ really took over. And we are still spending millions on these monuments today. [handwritten: Roman Church? Or Pagan Rome?]

3. The _"one pastor runs everything"_ model is totally _unscriptural._ Far from running everything, in the book of Acts we find the word [handwritten: Key] _"pastor" NOT EVEN USED ONCE._ (The early church did have [handwritten: Eph. 4:11] strong leaders and _elders._ But it was never a _"one man band"_ like we see today. And never was it so _"controlling" either)._

4. _"Tithing"_ is not a New Testament practice at all. And it is being shamefully _abused_ by today's preachers. In the New Testament we are told to _give cheerfully_ – whatever we purpose in our hearts to give. Telling people that they MUST give 10% to the church or they are "robbing God" is totally _sick_ – and a _money-grubbing_ way _of twisting Scripture._ There is no evidence that the apostles EVER preached 'tithing' to New Testament believers. It was clearly regarded as an Old Testament practice.

5. The words _"prosper" or "prosperity"_ were _NEVER used by Jesus at all_ – and only exist a couple of times in the entire New Testament. Yet greedy preachers have built whole kingdoms upon them. The words – _"sell what you have and give to the poor"_ and _"deceitfulness of riches"_ and _"you cannot serve God and mammon"_ and _"woe to you that are rich"_ were DEFINITELY used by Jesus and the apostles. But we don't hear these things preached too much, do we?

6. There were _no Bible Colleges, Seminaries or degrees_ in the New Testament. The only people who seemed to have "Bible Schools" were the _Scribes and Pharisees!_ The apostles were simple fishermen and tax collectors. It is likely that a number of them

could not even read or write. What was their "qualification" for being in the ministry? Simply that they had SPENT A LOT OF TIME WITH JESUS. The fact that people expect a "professional clergy" today with degrees from Bible College has helped to make the church sicker and more unscriptural than ever. Simple humble people with a calling from God often cannot get to minister because they do not have a "piece of paper" to make them 'qualified'. Yet another disaster for the church.

7. There is almost no evidence whatsoever that the early church had their "main meeting" on a Sunday. They gathered together 'from house to house' virtually every day! There were no church buildings. They did not dress up and "go to church". There were no denominations. There were no separate groups with different 'labels'. They lived their lives together – all the Christians in the local area. Love and fellowship and 'koinonia' were as natural to them as breathing. And the apostles in Jerusalem preached every day at huge open-air gatherings. Not "hidden away" inside four walls. This was truly a "street church" in every way.

8. The idea that you can replace the moving of the Holy Spirit with programs, programs and more programs just shows how low we have sunk. Man-made programs are everywhere today. The early church had much more of God and much less of 'man'.

9. We preach a 'humanistic' Jesus today. A Jesus who exists mainly for our own "happiness". A Santa Claus who wants to rain down continual blessings upon us. A God of grace and mercy without judgement, righteousness or truth. Our gross misrepresentation of who Jesus really is is one of the most serious offenses of the modern church. Today's church seems to worship a "plastic" Jesus. – one that she has made, in her own image. What an offense to God.

A lot of preachers are well aware that there is something very wrong with the church today. They know there is little 'fear of the Lord'. They know there is no deep repentance or deep moving of the Holy Spirit. They know that it is just the same old "game" being played every week. A lot of them are very aware of this. But they will not do anything about it. They will not rock the boat. And they will "squash" anyone who comes along trying to do something. They do not want a real "shaking". There is too much to lose. They have their careers and their little 'kingdoms' at stake. This is the real truth of the matter. This is where the rubber truly meets the road.

That is why God is about to bring "Great Reformation". He will not put up with these 'hirelings' any longer. He will not have them as leaders over His people. A lot of them are about to "lose their heads". They will never lead God's people again.

This is what true 'Reformation' is all about. It is the process of replacing the old leadership and the old lies. It is David taking over from 'Saul'.

There is a 'New Wineskin' coming. In fact it is upon us. There is a new leadership arising – many of them trained in the 'wilderness' for such a time as this. The hour is now here. LET THE NEW LEADERS ARISE! The sad fact is that today's church has sunk so low that it is almost a matter of people needing to be RESCUED OUT OF HER. I never thought I would say something as radical as that, but it is the truth.

Much of the church is living a lie. Many inside her are told continuously that they are "OK" – that they are saved and headed for heaven. Nothing could be further from the truth. Multitudes of them are headed directly for hell. The systemized LYING that is going on has deceived the leaders and the people alike. It is the blind leading the blind. We need to contend for these people – desperately. Much of the church is "lost". They are mired in deception – an entire system of deception.

Wow! That one sure set the cat amongst the pigeons! Now you can see why I was bombarded with emails for weeks, both "for" and against the statements made above. But it was only in ensuing weeks that I was able to deal with each issue individually, and finally give more clarity and scriptural backing for each one.

Amidst some of the more vitriolic replies, it was refreshing to receive this one from a scholar whom I will identify simply as "Dr Adrian": *"I loved your article Andrew, and I think it is absolutely spot on. Even although I am a pastor and I also teach theology in a Bible school :-) I do try to teach them good stuff. I have been teaching ecclesiology this term, and many of the things you have said are recognised even by very conservative evangelical theologians as being completely biblical, New Testament truth. Unfortunately, some of them then try to explain away why it is not like that now!"*

This first article was mainly to generate interest in the series that was to follow. And it certainly did its job well! From now on in this book, we will be looking at each of these issues individually, beginning with the whole question of "Asking Jesus into our heart".

CHAPTER THREE

"ASKING JESUS INTO OUR HEART"??

One of the most basic things that has amazed me for many years is the preaching of "Giving your heart to the Lord" or "Asking Jesus into your life" to become a Christian. Do we not realize that such a practice is found NOWHERE in the entire Bible? Is there ANY example of someone "asking Jesus into their heart" (or similar) to become a Christian in the book of Acts? NO – NOT EVEN ONE. The book of Acts is full of literally thousands of people becoming born-again Christians. And we are often told exactly what these people did. But there is no record of any of them doing anything like "asking Jesus into their heart" to be saved.

Now surely, this has got to be one of the most crucial and basic points in the whole New Testament: How exactly are people supposed to become Christians? What were they told to do in the New Testament? A very simple and straight-forward question, you would think.

But when we are asked, "What shall we DO TO BE SAVED?" today, our answer is almost always TOTALLY different from that of the apostles. Incredible really, isn't it? In the Bible it is right there in black-and-white, time after time! But TRADITION has blinded our eyes to the Truth. And I'm sure that even many of you reading this will be shocked at how obvious the truth of this matter is. Let's start with the day of Pentecost (a great place to begin!). As we all know, the Holy Spirit fell on the 120, and they all began to speak in tongues. This is officially known by theologians as the birth of the Church – the beginning of Christianity as we know it. And after Peter preached his convicting sermon to the gathered crowd that day, another 3,000 people were added to the church. And we are told exactly what occurred: "... They were cut to the heart, and said to Peter and the other apostles, 'Brothers, WHAT

SHALL WE DO?' Peter replied, 'REPENT and be BAPTIZED, every one of you, in the name of Jesus Christ for the FORGIVENESS OF YOUR SINS. And you shall receive the gift of the HOLY SPIRIT'" (Acts 2:37-38, NIV). Notice how different Peter's reply is to what we tell people today. We might have said something like, "Just say this little prayer after me" but Peter said nothing like that at all.

There were three elements to what Peter told them: ① REPENTANCE, ③ WATER-BAPTISM and receiving the HOLY ② SPIRIT. We see this pattern repeated again and again, right through the book of Acts (in fact, throughout the New Testament writings) in the most glaringly obvious way. And yet still we hear, "Just ask Jesus into your heart" preached throughout Christendom today. The next significant people-group to be reached by the early Christians were the Samaritans. In Acts chapter 8 we read how Philip the evangelist saw massive Revival in Samaria: "But when they believed Philip as he preached the good news of the kingdom of God and the name of Jesus Christ, they were BAPTIZED, both men and women.... they sent Peter and John to them. When they arrived, they prayed for them that they might RECEIVE THE HOLY SPIRIT" (Acts 8:12-17). Note the identical pattern to the salvations on the day of Pentecost.

I hope you realize that we have been talking about THOUSANDS of conversions here. And NOT ONE of them involved "Giving their heart to the Lord" or "Inviting Jesus to be their personal savior". If you look up these Scriptures in Acts, you will see that every time it was "Repentance, Baptism and Receiving the Holy Spirit". Over and over again.

The next significant people-group to be reached by the early church were the 'Godly' gentiles (Acts chapters 10 and 11). Peter was led to preach to Cornelius and his household. And God suddenly moved even while he was still preaching!: "While Peter was still speaking these words, the HOLY SPIRIT CAME on all who heard the message... For they heard them SPEAKING IN TONGUES and praising God. Then Peter said, 'Can anyone keep these people from being BAPTIZED with water? They have RECEIVED THE HOLY SPIRIT just as we have.' So he ordered that they be baptized in the name of Jesus Christ" (Acts 10:44-48). Peter later described these people as having been "Baptized in the Holy Spirit" (Acts 11:16). I hope you can see from these passages that the Holy Spirit 'COMING UPON' people is the same experience as them 'RECEIVING' or being 'BAPTIZED' in the Holy Spirit. Thus we see the same pattern as before, in the salvation experience of Cornelius' household – 1) Repentant hearts, 2) Receiving the Holy Spirit and 3) Baptism. 3 *before 2 ?*

Another good example involves some disciples of John the Baptist whom Paul met at Ephesus: "Paul said, 'John's baptism was a baptism of REPENTANCE. He told the people to believe in the one coming after him, that is, in Jesus.' On hearing this, they were BAPTIZED into the name of the Lord Jesus. When Paul placed his hands on them, the HOLY SPIRIT came on them, and they SPOKE IN TONGUES and prophesied" (Acts 19:1-6). I guess I hardly need to point out the pattern by now?

Notice too that there were no "instructional classes" to prepare people for baptism. All the way through the book of Acts, people were baptized STRAIGHT AWAY, as soon as they were believing and repentant. With the Philippian jailer, he and his entire household were baptized immediately – IN THE MIDDLE OF THE NIGHT (Acts 16:32-33). With the Ethiopian eunuch, he was baptized by Philip straight away, in some water that they saw while travelling in his chariot (Acts 8:35-38). And the apostle Paul himself was baptized immediately by the disciple Ananias, who said something very interesting to Paul beforehand: "Be BAPTIZED and WASH YOUR SINS AWAY, calling on His name" (Acts 22:16). This verse would be treated almost like → "heresy" by many in today's church. How shocking to imply that baptism might have something to do with forgiveness and cleansing from our past sins! However, there are many verses like it scattered throughout the New Testament. Also note that Paul was told this DAYS AFTER he had had his blinding 'Damascus Road' experience. Today's Christians might assume that Paul was "born

- 17 -

again" during that blinding encounter with God. Not so. Not until Paul was to be BAPTIZED was he to have his sins "washed away". This is clearly what the Scriptures say – arguments anyone?

Many Christians are taught today that Baptism is basically a 'symbolic' act. In my youth I was raised mainly in (Baptist) churches, and they always taught that baptism is an "outward SYMBOL of an inner change". Thus baptism is stripped of much of its significance and power in Christian thinking. For a "symbol" is never as important as the real thing, is it? I have studied baptism extensively in the New Testament. It is NEVER spoken of as a mere 'SYMBOL'. Rather, it is spoken of as being a 'circumcision of the heart', a "cutting off", a "burial" into the DEATH of Christ. And it is also spoken of as being "for the forgiveness of sins" and to "wash one's sins away". I am convinced that in the spirit-realm (from God's point of view), baptism is seen as a LITERAL "burial into death" (see Romans 6) which has a profound effect on our hearts and lives. But still we preach, "Ask Jesus into your heart", and deny many people one of the most vital keys to living a Christian life. I am also convinced that baptism MUST be by 'FULL IMMERSION'. Sprinkling little infants is not enough. This must be baptism for BELIEVERS. And the original Greek word 'baptizo' actually means "TO DIP OR IMMERSE". So people must be 'buried' under the water in baptism, not just sprinkled. (I'm sure most of you already agree with this).

Likewise I am convinced that Baptism in the Holy Spirit (accompanied by 'speaking in tongues') is ESSENTIAL. It is NOT just an option. As we have seen in the book of Acts, the way that people became Christians in the New Testament was to 1) Repent, 2) Be baptized in water and 3) Be baptized in the Holy Spirit (accompanied by 'tongues' as far as we can tell). What right do we have to change the fundamental teachings and practices of the Bible, just so we can make things more "convenient" for new converts? Unless we are getting people saved the Bible way, how can we claim to be getting them saved at all?

We are forever talking about being "born again" in the church

- 18 -

today. But are we truly getting people 'born again' like they did in Acts? Bearing in mind the pattern that we have seen in the New Testament, what exactly do you think Jesus was talking about when He declared that, "No-one can enter the kingdom of God unless he is born of WATER and THE SPIRIT"? (Jn 3:5, NIV).

Whatever Jesus meant by those words, one thing we do know is that baptism in water and the Spirit are never regarded as mere 'options' in the Scriptures. In fact they are clearly ESSENTIAL experiences to begin to walk in Christ's kingdom. There are many Scriptures on this that are often bypassed today or regarded as "inexplicable" because they do not fit in with current tradition. Please take the time to look up the following: Mark 16:16-18, 1 Peter 3:20-21, Titus 3:5-6, 1 Cor 10:1-2, Gal 3:27, Col 2:11-12, 1 Cor 12:13, Heb 6:1-2, Rom 6:2-11, Rom 8:9, Mt 28:19, etc.

I really mean it. Please do take the time to look at the above Scriptures if you have any interest in this issue at all. Many people write to me with their opinions, saying, "I cannot believe you are teaching this." And yet they have never bothered to actually look up the Scriptures on the subject! PLEASE read Acts and look up the above Scriptures before sending me your views.

It is my belief that there are a number of important teachings and practices from the early church that will be restored during the coming Revival. (God often does this in Revivals). I am convinced that the above teaching will be one of them. (I have believed this for many years).

I realize that I have probably shocked and provoked a number of you with this chapter. Please believe me, I myself was very shocked when I first came face-to-face with these truths some years ago. They really are very apparent when you study them, but I was blind to them for many years. I was amongst those who gave out tracts like 'The Four Spiritual Laws' and led people in the "sinner's prayer". Like many, I would back this up by misapplying Rev 3:20 – "Behold I stand at the door and knock. If any man hear my voice and open the door I will come in to him, and sup with him and he with me." It was only later that I realized that, as Leonard Ravenhill points out, this Scripture is clearly aimed at the CHURCH, not at unconverted sinners. It is Jesus standing outside the 'Laodicean' church, trying to get in! Please go and read the whole passage – Rev 3:14-21. You will see what I mean. It is very clear.

I am not ashamed that I used to preach these things. It was all I knew at the time. But I was certainly shocked to discover how much of the basic gospel I was leaving out. Like me, there are a number of you who will have to "search the Scriptures to see if these things be so" just as the Bereans did. Believe me, I fought these truths for months before I simply ran out of corners to back into. I knew the implications of this were huge and I just did not want to face it. But there they are in black and white. And this is not a trivial matter. These are key gospel truths that we are talking about here.

After writing the first version of this article, many people wrote to me pointing out that the THIEF ON THE CROSS was not baptized or Spirit-filled, yet he was clearly saved. Well, I had all these same objections when I first came across this teaching. But God annihilated all my excuses one by one. So let me deal with this "THIEF ON THE CROSS" thing right here.

The most obvious question is: When did this event occur – was it under the OLD Covenant or the NEW Covenant? When Jesus proffered salvation to the thief, was the Old Covenant still in place, or had the New begun? For clearly, it only became possible to become an actual CHRISTIAN (born again – a member of Christ's body) AFTER the New Covenant had started. And for the New Covenant to begin, Jesus, the sacrificial Lamb had to die and also be RAISED FROM THE DEAD. The New Covenant could not begin until this occurred. Surely we all know this? Jesus had to die and be raised from the dead, and then ascend into heaven, sending His Holy Spirit, before the Church could truly begin or people could start becoming born-again Christians. That is why people in the Old Testament, or even in Jesus' own day were not "born again" the way we are today. They simply couldn't be. Remember, Jesus said that John the Baptist was the greatest born among men, but even the least in the kingdom was greater than he. John the Baptist couldn't become a "born-again Christian" because the New Covenant had not yet begun. I bet he would have loved the opportunity! Jesus died in agony and was raised again, to purchase for us this wonderful new life in Him. Surely we all know this? GLORY TO GOD!!

Now back to the thief. Did he have his conversation with Jesus and die under the New Covenant or the Old? The answer, obviously, is: The OLD Covenant. He was presumably a Jew – one of God's chosen people (though a sinner), who received a wonderful pardon from Jesus when he repented and turned to Him. But those were very different conditions to those that we live under today. We now have a NEW Covenant – a NEW "agreement" with God, very different from the Old. We have a new and living way in which to walk. How do we enter into it? By being born again – of water and the Spirit. And this has only been possible since Pentecost – the day the church began. I am not saying that "death-bed repentance" is not possible today. I'm sure that God has reached down in His mercy many times to people who have turned to Him when they were close to death. But these are special cases. They are not the "norm" for New Testament Christianity. Repentance, Baptism and receiving the Holy Spirit are ESSENTIAL to enter into the New Covenant, I believe.

As I said, many people offer me their own views and opinions on all this without truly studying the basic Scriptures on the matter. It is important to remember that fundamental doctrines are not about mere opinion. They are about what the SCRIPTURES SAY. I tell you, I have put MONTHS of study and prayer into this whole subject. I could tell that it really was THAT important. I honestly considered EVERYTHING – every angle I could find. Please treat this with the seriousness that it is due. This is a very crucial area. I believe these are SALVATION issues that are being discussed here. And the case is enormously strong. Just read the Scriptures. (It should take less than an hour to read through the Scriptures highlighted above). I urge any of you who are the least bit interested in this to PLEASE read those Scriptures.

I am well aware that 'doctrine' tends to be divisive by its very nature. And I know that I am taking a big risk talking so openly about such a controversial teaching. I try and keep right away from doctrinal debates in general. It is only the most fundamental and important issues that I bother making a fuss about. You will notice that even though I run a 'Prophetic' website, there are no debates about the 'Pre-trib'/ Post-trib positions or the exact meaning of Daniel's 70 weeks, etc. I just find such debates pointless and utterly dull, to be honest. I heard the arguments many moons ago, and just cannot stomach any more. I have no desire for nit-picking arguments. But the BIG issues, like New Testament salvation and God's plan for His church – these things I really do care about. For I believe the devil is robbing us blind in some of these crucial areas. And God wants to restore these truths to the church.

Just imagine for a moment that I am right, and baptism and receiving the Holy Spirit are a lot more important than we have been led to believe. Just think how many thousands of believers around the world today have received the Holy Spirit (including 'tongues') but have simply not bothered getting baptized. After all, it's only "symbolic", right? Or perhaps they say, "I got sprinkled as a baby." I myself know many people in this exact position. I think it's terrible, and I believe God does too. Not to mention all the believers who still have not been baptized in the Holy Spirit. Don't you think God's heart aches over all this? Why do people ignore His commands? Our church traditions and habitual patterns have a lot to answer for in this area. This has got to change, my friends. And I believe it will only change when the underlying doctrines are challenged. But if I am right, the devil will fight this all the way. He likes anything that leaves believers impoverished or still chained up in any way. This really is crucial doctrine, otherwise I simply would not bother with it. I have really stuck my neck on the line and risked my reputation over this. And I do not do so lightly.

I have been accused of being "legalistic" and 'majoring on minor points' by a couple of readers. I really cannot see this. As I have said, some doctrine is "straining at gnats" and some is really crucial. I believe this issue falls into the second category. Others accused me of being "too literal"! (I had to laugh over this). Now this is basic Bible doctrine we are talking about here, isn't it? Too literal? What on earth else should we be?

Other readers accused me of believing in "baptismal regeneration". This is not the case. I believe that 1) Repentance, 2) Water-Baptism and 3) Receiving the Holy Spirit, are ALL ESSENTIAL. I do not believe in "baptismal" regeneration. These elements are all equally important and we need to have all three to be able to call ourselves 'New Testament Christians', as far as I can see.

Other readers have brought up the verse in Romans that says "If you confess with your mouth, 'Jesus is Lord,' and believe in your heart that God raised Him from the dead, you will be saved" (Rom 10:9, NIV). Actually, a number of theologians believe that this statement was used as a kind of "baptismal confession" in the early church. I remember a fellowship I was involved with years ago that used it in exactly this way. To me, this verse "proves" little doctrinally, either way. It needs to be put into context with the WHOLE New Testament to gain the proper perspective on it. I certainly don't see it as proof for 'asking Jesus into our heart'.

One of the most serious allegations I have faced is that I am preaching a kind of "justification by works" by saying that baptism and receiving the Holy Spirit are so essential. And that I am "adding to the gospel" and taking away people's freedom like the Galatians!! Serious charges, indeed. But let's look at this carefully. Is baptism a "work" that I can do to myself? Is receiving the Holy Spirit a "work"? I don't think so! These are initial experiences that are 'DONE TO US' or given to us – they're not things that we can "DO" ourselves, as such. Can I baptize myself? No! And isn't it a brief one-off act of simple faith and obedience anyway? To me, baptism is no more a "work" than, say, the act of "praying a sinner's prayer". The act of opening one's mouth, moving one's jaws and praying is not seen as a work. And neither should baptism be. They only take an instant, after all. The real question is: Is baptism a truly spiritual act, or is it merely a symbolic ritual? That is the real question. This also brings up the whole issue of 'convenience'. For we love neat little packages that are comfortable and easy in this age, don't we? ("Just asking Jesus in"). And baptism is so wet and messy, we think. But at the end of the day, what it boils down to is this: We have to make a decision between doing things the Bible way and doing things the modern 'convenient' way. It is that simple.

Now, onto something else that numerous people raised: Where does FAITH come into all this? Aren't we supposed to be saved by FAITH? Absolutely! And faith is at a premium right through this whole thing. What happens when someone hears the gospel and BELIEVES it? (A crucially important moment). Are they automatically a 'Christian' now? Just through believing what they have heard? Or do they have to act on that belief in some way to become a Christian? Were the Jews who were 'cut to the heart' when Peter preached at Pentecost automatically Christians right then at that moment, or did they have to DO something in FAITH to become Christians? Clearly, they needed to DO something, because Peter told them, "Repent and be baptized, and you will receive the gift of the Holy Spirit." And it is clear that each one of these elements involves the exercise of faith in Jesus.

However, I believe that when the Bible speaks of the "faith that saves us", and being "JUSTIFIED BY FAITH", it is speaking of the LIFE OF FAITH that we undertake after we have become a Christian. It is 'WALKING IN FAITH' day by day, moment by moment, after having become a Christian that justifies us before God. It is the covering of the blood of Jesus that hides our sin and makes us clean in God's sight. If we are walking in faith, covered by the blood, we are saved, and we must continue to walk in it. And it is clear in the Scriptures that it is only by the POWER OF THE HOLY SPIRIT that we can walk in this kind of saving faith. This faith is a gift from God – "Not of ourselves... lest anyone should boast." Like the love of God, this faith is shed abroad in our hearts by the Holy Spirit, who is given to us. So how can we obtain it without RECEIVING THE HOLY SPIRIT? (Which brings us) back to Repentance, Baptism and Receiving the Holy Spirit as our ESSENTIAL starting point in the faith).

Actually, a couple of readers mentioned something quite interesting about baptism in the book of Acts. For it is noticeable in Acts that everyone was baptized "IN THE NAME OF THE LORD JESUS" or in the 'NAME OF JESUS CHRIST'. Now most churches today baptize in the name of the 'Father, Son and Holy Spirit', and I guess this is a small point, but I believe that if they felt it was important in Acts to speak the name of Jesus Christ over people as they were baptized, then I should do it too. I am not legalistic about the need for this, but personally these days I baptize people "in the name of the Father and the Son and the Holy Spirit, in the NAME OF JESUS CHRIST". (To make sure all the bases are covered). *Note!*

WHO IS QUALIFIED TO BAPTIZE?

The simple truth, as found in Scripture, is that we are ALL "kings and priests" and there is absolutely nothing to prevent any Spirit-filled believer at all from baptizing someone else. In fact, Paul himself was baptized by a simple "disciple" named Ananias – not by some great leader

I was 20 years old (and certainly not "ordained" or anything) when God led me to begin baptizing people. It has truly been my joy to baptize dozens and dozens since then. One time when I was 23 I was in Fiji on a mission trip accompanying a more senior evangelist, and one night in Suva the Holy Spirit really began to move. There was no-one else to do it, so I was asked to walk down to the beach in the middle of the night (pitch-black) and baptize seven people in the ocean! I have to say, I have never felt closer to the book of Acts than I did that night. Another time I got a phone call asking me to baptize about 23 people in a swimming pool. Again, it was a feeling uncannily like the Book of Acts that I had that day. This is exactly the kind of thing that we are missing in the church! The feeling that we "could be in Acts"! We almost never feel that way. And yet most of the things we are missing are very simple

I tell you, when "ordinary" Christians begin to do the simple things, like baptize people in bathtubs and rivers and break bread in their homes and move in the gifts of the Spirit – THAT is when the sense of "being in Acts" can sweep in again. And anything can happen. Christianity actually becomes EXCITING.

Releasing the whole body to be involved in these things is very important. That is what "tomorrow's church" will be all about.

So we need to start challenging our friends and asking them some simple questions that we have not thought to ask them before. Like, "Have you been baptized?".... And "Would you like to be??"

no, most poured

IN SUMMARY

It is my belief that God has been slowly restoring truth to the church over the centuries since the Dark Ages when so much had been lost. Luther's Reformation saw the restoration of 'Justification by Faith', the Anabaptists reintroduced baptism by immersion, Wesley reintroduced the importance of the 'new birth', and this century the Pentecostals rediscovered the infilling of the Holy Spirit and spiritual gifts. (There have been many other things over time also, but this is just a simple overview). It is my belief that we are now at the stage where God wishes to restore the church to her true original glory, with all the basic doctrines and practices, "church life" and the full original gospel, the 'five-fold' ministries, etc. – Everything. That is what is about to occur in the coming Revival, I believe. And that is another reason why I believe basic New Testament doctrines are so important.

In past centuries, as now, the believers of that time walked in the light that they had, and God will judge them according to the light that was available to them. But now it is time to see the church truly restored to fullness in many areas. And it is going to be UNCOMFORTABLE, and it will surely leave much "SHAKEN" in its wake. A new Reformation is coming, and it is important that it leaves nothing undone that needs doing. Otherwise our children are going to have to have a further Reformation to correct all that we left undone. Let's make it as complete as possible this time, shall we? For Christ cannot return until a glorious Bride is made ready for Him, without "spot or wrinkle or any such thing". Surely we live in the days of the 'restoration of all things' about which the Scriptures speak.

REPLIES FROM READERS

Naturally I received a huge number of emails relating to the above article. But one thing I noticed was that only a relatively small number said they had actually LOOKED UP the Scriptures that I quoted. Now, you will be amazed if you actually do this. In fact, if you read the entire Book of Acts, taking careful note of EVERY born-again experience and what happened, then you will be amazed the same way. Another thing you can do when studying this kind of issue is get a Concordance and look up EVERY Scripture on 'Baptism' and so-on. I encourage everybody to do this kind of thing. None of this is about our own "opinions". It is about what the SCRIPTURES CLEARLY SAY on the subject. Below are several replies from people who did look into the Scriptures on this matter:

Rachel H. wrote:

I want to thank you so much for your article on Lie # 1 – "Ask Jesus Into Our Heart". I was raised in a Baptist church also, so this is all new to me. I was skeptical at first, but I looked up every single verse in that article, and I have to say, WOW! I never knew that baptism played such an important role in becoming a Christian! I was baptized at a young age, but that was only because I had said that famous short prayer to accept Jesus into my heart, and attended the baptismal preparation classes!

I know that now, 13 years later, it's time to be truly baptized.

You covered every area, most of which I have never even known about, thank you so much!

I would also like to share something that God had revealed to me a couple of months ago about churches and the body of Christ. It started after I read a book about a revival that had taken place in Africa in the 50's. The key factor to their revival was REPENTANCE. When the people realized that Jesus had died for their sins, and they truly believed, they began repenting, confessing sins out loud, in front of large groups of people!

They weren't doing it for show, many times they were crying and moaning, sickened at their own sins but desperate to get it out. There was such a spirit of conviction there, that some of the people, as poor as they were, began repaying money that they had stolen years before that, or giving back eggs and animals that they had wrongfully taken. They were asking for forgiveness from other people left and right for things they had thought or said in anger and hate. Some of the people tried to keep their sins in, and they actually got physically sick until that sin was confessed. Some of the sins were more serious, but sin is sin to God, right?

What God revealed to me about churches is that everyone has some hidden sin that they don't want anyone to know about. Even the pastors and elders are hiding sin that they don't want to share, because, of course, they don't want to be looked down upon! God showed me that people need to confess their sins, they need to be truly repentant of them for there to be any kind of revival.

Pastor David K. wrote:

Bro Andrew Strom, thank you for your response on the first of nine – "ASK JESUS into our Heart".

You have opened my eyes on this one. I have read your article line by line and verse by verse. You have turned my heart. I will watch with the same interest for the other eight. I see your position and on this point concede, I have been trained more by tradition than by the Word.

Ian J. wrote:

Having just returned from India I must make the following observations re-salvation.

To be a Christian in the churches that I ministered in means a turning away from the old gods and destroying of all idols. They regard people as seekers of truth at this stage, but it's not until they are Baptised in Water which is usually followed by an infilling of the Holy Spirit that they are regarded as Christian. I want to tell you that there is a tremendous cost to being publicly baptised. Often it is accompanied by a separation of familiy members who refuse to accept that they have become Christians. The truth is that if a Hindu comes to Church he is not persecuted, but the moment a decision is made to be baptised "all Hell" breaks loose. Because what is happening is more than symbolic, it is an act of covenant. A demonstration of alliegance to a Kingdom.

Brian J. wrote:

Rev. David Pawson from England has written a book and done a video, both entitled "The Normal Christian Birth." Both are in line with your position. David speaks of repentance towards God, faith in Jesus, baptism in water and the infilling of the Holy Spirit as the steps involved in the "Normal Christian Birth", based on the accounts in the Book of Acts.

Anchor Recordings summarise it as follows: "So often, spiritual disease can be traced back to an inadequate initiation into the Kingdom. A better birth means greater growth in a healthy Christian life. David Pawson discusses some crucial and controversial biblical texts, challenging many traditional interpretations. He questions the adequacy of the typical "sinners prayer" approach and gives practical tips on helping potential disciples to repent, believe, be baptised and receive the Holy Spirit."

Perhaps those who argue against might like to read the book or get hold of the video themselves. In the UK both are available from – http://www.anchor-recordings.com

FURTHER BIBLE STUDY:

Acts 1:8, Acts 2:1-4, Acts 2:37-41, Acts 8:12-20, Acts 10:44-48, Acts 11:15-18, Acts 19:1-6, Acts 22:16, Matt 3:13-16, John 3:5, Heb 6:1-2, Mark 16:16-18, 1 Peter 3:20-21, Titus 3:5-6, 1 Cor 10:1-2, Gal 3:27, Col 2:11-12, 1 Cor 12:13, Rom 6:2-11, Rom 8:9, Matt 28:19.

CHAPTER FOUR

CHURCH BUILDINGS

Here is a simple statement of fact to start this chapter: Church buildings are not in the Bible – Period. They simply do not exist. They are another invention of man. You can search the entire New Testament from beginning to end and you will find no mention of them at all. It was only after two centuries, when the church was slowly giving way to apostasy and deception, that church buildings began to appear. Even then, they were often just two houses joined together. It was not until after 300AD, when the church fell into Roman apostasy that "cathedrals" began to be built.

A lot of people think that us having church buildings today "doesn't really matter". They say buildings are kind-of 'neutral'. That they don't really affect us. They are just a building, after all. But I disagree strongly with this. I believe there is a whole mindset and a whole pattern of "learnt behavior" that goes with church buildings – especially in the West. We find this difficult to see, because we are so used to them.

Below are some brief quotes from scholars and historians who have looked into this subject:

"'We have no temples or altars.' This statement, referring to Christians, comes from the pen of the apologist Minicus Felix, c 200, and all evidence supports its accuracy. Throughout at least the first two centuries there were no church buildings as such." (J.G. Davies).

"When the church was very young, it had no buildings. Let us begin with that striking fact. That the church had no buildings is the most noticeable of the points of difference between the church of the early days and the church of today. In the minds

of most people today, "church" means first a building, probably something else second; but seldom does "the church" stand for anything other than a building. Yet here is the fact with which we start: the early church possessed no buildings and carried on its work for a great many years without erecting any." (Ernest Loosley).

"The church's greatest period of vitality and growth until recent times was during the first two centuries A.D. In other words, the church grew fastest when it did not have the help or hindrance of church buildings." (Howard Snyder).

Isn't this a remarkable thing? Here we are in the 21st Century, still pouring so much money and pain and sacrifice into our buildings – and yet the whole concept is not even in the Bible!

So how did the early believers gather together then? Well, there are two answers to this. A lot of people in the "house church" movement will tell you that the early Christians simply met in homes. They are right, but that is only half the story. For in the early church in Jerusalem they not only met in homes, but the apostles also held massive OPEN-AIR meetings every day. Huge public gatherings.

Where did they hold these great open-air meetings? In and around a place called "Solomon's Porch" – which was in the most crowded and well-travelled part of Jerusalem. In fact, it was right "in the face" of hundreds and thousands of people passing by on foot. Solomon's Porch was in the 'Courtyard of the Gentiles' which was a huge open courtyard attached to the main Temple. In a lot of ways it served as the "town square" of Jerusalem. Hundreds upon hundreds of people passed through it every day. And there they could see the apostles, teaching and healing the sick right in front of the whole world. What a great place for Revival meetings!! (Actually, this is where Jesus preached when He was in Jerusalem also).

That is why I talk so often about an "outdoor church" and a "street revival". The fact of the matter is that the original church WAS an 'outdoor church'. But you would never know it looking at today's church, would you? What we do today is hide ourselves away from the world – behind 'four walls' (which usually cost a fortune to build). How sad – And how unscriptural. Jesus' ministry was mostly in the open air. John the Baptist's ministry was very much in the open air. The Book of Acts church in Jerusalem was mostly in the open air. But we are the very opposite. And it is costing us millions each year to erect more "walls". No wonder we don't impact the world like we should!

Apart from the huge outdoor gatherings, the only other place that the early believers seemed to meet was in homes. There they would gather most days, sharing their lives with one another. Eating and taking communion together, praying, operating spiritual gifts and teaching new converts. A whole lifestyle of love and community, that is what the early church was like – And no "church buildings" in sight.

Read this carefully (Acts 2:42-46, NIV): "They devoted themselves to the apostles' teaching and to the fellowship, to the breaking of bread and to prayer. Everyone was filled with awe and many wonders and miraculous signs were done by the apostles. All the believers were together and had everything in common... Every day they continued to meet together in the temple courts. They broke bread in their homes and ate together with glad and sincere hearts." (See also Acts 4:32-35, Acts 5:12-16, etc).

So it was 1) The temple courtyard and 2) Houses where they met. Now we can see why, all the way through the New Testament, Paul speaks about the "church that meets in so-and-so's house": "To Archippus our fellow soldier and to the church that meets in YOUR HOME" (Phile v 2); "Aquila and Priscilla great you warmly in the Lord, and so does the church that meets at THEIR HOUSE" (1 Cor 16:19. See also Rom 16:5, Col 4:15, etc). When you really look into it, you discover that the New Testament Church was simply one huge network of house churches – all united "as one". These were not independent fellowships or denominations. They were "one church" – one body – under the leadership of the apostles. No divisions or separations at all. How very different from today.

When we talk about outdoor meetings, a lot of people start asking questions like, "But what happens when the weather is bad?" or "What do we do during winter?" The answer is pretty simple: We hire a warehouse or a stadium or something for 4 months and go out again when the weather improves. We also have our HOMES to gather in, all year round. Actually, I believe it is likely that when the coming Revival gains momentum, we may find that STADIUMS become the most logical place to gather on a consistent basis – all year round. There have been a number of dreams and visions of the coming move of God that show this occurring.

Remember, the early church was very PRACTICAL about such things. If you need to hire some place then by all means do so! God is not "hung up" about where we meet. But we must never forget the pattern established in the Jerusalem church. I believe it is going to become very important in the coming Revival. In fact, I am convinced that we are about to see a powerful move of God and a great 'SHAKING' in the church, that will bring her into the kind of glorious, united, OUTDOOR Christianity that we have been talking about here. Personally, I can't wait!

TEMPLE & SYNAGOGUES

Quite a few people wrote to me asking about "synagogues". Well, it is clear that both Jesus and the apostles went into the Jewish synagogues to preach to the JEWS. For awhile they were able to get away with preaching in there, but eventually the persecution got so bad that they were unable to do so. But these synagogues were never "Christian" buildings at all. They were part of the Jewish system and the apostles went in there to preach to the Jews. It was an 'outreach'. There is no record of them EVER building their own "Christian synagogues"!

A number of people also seemed confused about the 'Temple' in Jerusalem, for the Bible often speaks of Jesus or the apostles "teaching in the temple". As I said earlier, the part of the temple where they taught was called 'Solomon's Porch', which was a narrow (45-foot wide) porch-like overhang running right along one edge of the huge temple courtyard. Now, this 'porch' was quite interesting; the roof of it was almost four stories up in the air, held up by large columns, and it was big enough for the apostles to stand under it, and also for part of the crowd to get some shade and shelter by pressing in there too. However, because there were at least 7000 of them within a matter of days, most of the crowd must have been out in the open-air courtyard as they pressed in to hear the person who was speaking. The whole thing was quite open. But at least there was a little bit of shade and shelter down that end of the courtyard! This was the area where all the religious teachers and rabbis came to speak to the crowds who passed by every day. So it was a wonderful place for the apostles to preach. As I said, this courtyard was like a massive 'public square' – very busy.

So that is what it means when it says "Jesus taught in the temple". This was not some 'church building'! It was a very open public place. As one of my readers commented: *"I didn't know when the Scriptures referred to meeting in the temple, which was destroyed later, that they were meeting in the big area you described, and it wasn't so religious as but simply free for use, out in the open, and available as an excellent location."* Exactly! That's why it was so perfect to gather there.

So why do we hide ourselves away behind "four walls" today, my friends? Shouldn't we be "one church" right out in the open where the whole world can see and hear?

SOURCES:
-Ernest Loosley, "When The Church Was Young".
-J.G. Davies, "Secular Use of Church Buildings".
-Howard Snyder, "The Problem of Wineskins".
-Beckham, "Second Reformation".

- www.churchinfocus.org .
- Darryl M. Erkel, "Church Buildings or House-Churches?"
- www.housechurch.org , "Miscellaneous House Church Quotes".
- M. Brown, "Revolution in the Church".

REPLIES FROM READERS:

Rob wrote:

I would like to add my personal experience to this building issue. It concerns a fairly large church (1500 people) that was in my home city.

When I found the church it was vibrant and full of life. There were people there from all walks of life, and it showed. Business men in their suits, students in their jeans and t-shirts, mechanics in their overalls, and butchers in their soiled white clothes. People did not want to go to church in their soiled clothes, it just so happened that they only finished work in time to make a mad dash there. Not only people from all walks of life, but from all age groups too. Many older people were there, as were the middle aged and young families, and the youth were more than equally represented too. The thing about this church was that it was not a building. Every week the people would hire a high-school gymnasium hall, setting up chairs and the things needed for such a large gathering of people. It did not stay like this unfortunately, and it was not too long before we all moved into a newly erected building.

At first things started out fine, after all, we were still sitting on wooden chairs and still had a plain concrete floor covered in dust to walk on. That was at first, before the changes started to come. It was lauded as a good thing, as a step forward. Perhaps they did not see the changes that were happening, but the changes were two-fold – with the building, but also with the people.

- 36 -

When the chairs were padded and covered we were suddenly not allowed to put our feet upon them, nor could people in soiled clothes use them, they had to find a plastic chair and sit at the back. The clothing of the floor with carpet did much for the acoustics of the building but suddenly people were removing boots at the main entrance to preserve the look and prevent dragging mud over this new surface. It so happened that business shoes were much better for removing mud than workboots. The changes continued with new curtains, painted walls, and plush decorations. By the time the building was completed, it was a very rich and elegant place to visit. The problem was that we had lost all of the people who did not fit into this place. Those who were poor, or wore soiled clothes, or did not feel comfortable in such a plush environment had soon moved on, looking for a place that would allow them to be themselves and not force them into certain lifestyles. It was not that anyone actually said this specifically, but the style of the building and the decorations certainly said it very clearly. Not only these changes, but something else started to happen with those people that remained. Slowly the level of clothing began to change. People that used to wear t-shirts were starting to wear collared shirts. Those wearing collared shirts would wear business shirts, and the better dressed people were starting to wear suits. Even our pastor, the man that used to dress very casually, started wearing suits.

By the time I left, the people were wearing smart casual clothes and better, and many of the people that were in the church had now moved on. This new place with the fancy layout was not for them. The church changed too. It seemed the focus was not on God as much as it was on the building, on the activities of the church, and on the monetary need. By the time I left, the church had also split. I have always wondered if this would have been the same result had the church never moved from their hired hall.

Alan S. wrote:

Over the past several months my family and I have been helping some folks about two hours drive from our home. They had been meeting in their home for quite some time. They began to notice two things; they were outgrowing their living room and more unsaved people began coming.

After a little while the husband approached a local bar, that's right a bar. He shared with the owners about Jesus eating and drinking with publicans and sinners, about church in the market place. Amazingly the owners loved the idea and our friends started meeting there, in the bar, on Sunday evenings (at no cost). What followed is still amazing all of us. On any given Sunday night there are between 60-120 people showing up. The average number of non-Christians is around 30 with approximately 20-30 people being born again within the past 3-4 months. I, for one, have always believed that the church should be in the "market place". It's just great to see and experience it like this, IN A BAR!

FURTHER BIBLE STUDY:

Acts 5:42, Acts 17:17, John 16:1-2, John 12:42-43, Matt 10:17, Matt 23:34-35, Rev 2:9, Acts 7:48-49, John 10:22-24, Matt 26:55, Acts 19:8-10, Acts 3:11-12, Acts 5:12-16, Acts 5:19-21, Acts 2:46, Acts 4:32-35, 1 Cor 3:16-17, Phile v 2, 1 Cor 16:19, Rom 16:5, Col 4:15.

CHAPTER FIVE

THE "ONE MAN PASTOR" SYSTEM

Most churches today are run using the 'Senior Pastor' model, where one man (almost always with a degree from Bible College) does most of the ministering and is looked up to as "the man of God". Few could deny that pastors are truly the ones who are running the church today. (Though it could be argued in a number of places that the "big tithers" run the church – by keeping the pastor under their thumb!)

Personally, I get on well with a lot of pastors that I meet. I certainly recognize that it is a very stressful job. And I am also a strong upholder of godly leadership in the church. But I guess that writing on this topic will cause people to question my motives and accuse me of being "rebellious" and having 'problems with authority', etc. But honestly, this is not the case. I simply believe that it is time for us to examine the facts of this matter – and acquaint ourselves with what the Bible truly says.

Amazingly enough, in the Book of Acts, which is the history of the first 30 YEARS of the early church, the word 'Pastor' is NOT EVEN MENTIONED ONCE. Which is pretty astounding considering how often we use it today. In fact, even in the whole New Testament the word is only used rarely – especially when referring to ministry 'offices'. And when it does appear, it is found near the bottom of a list of ministries in the church: "It was he who gave some to be apostles, some to be prophets, some to be evangelists, and some to be pastors and teachers..." (Eph 4:11, NIV).

There were elders and 'overseers' (these terms are interchangeable) in the New Testament church. But that is quite different from the position of "one man pastor" that we have today.

So how did Pastors end up running everything? And what effect does this have on the church?

Well, when you study history it becomes obvious that we mostly got this concept from Rome – not from the Bible. As Beckham said: *"Emporer Constantine developed a church structure that has lasted for seventeen centuries... People go to a building (cathedral) on a special day of the week (Sunday) and someone (a priest, or today, a pastor) does something to them (teaching, preaching, absolution or healing) or for them (a ritual or entertainment) for a price (offerings)."*

In most cases, what we are seeing today is the continuation of this "Clergy and Laity" system that dominated the church during the Dark Ages. There is very little difference, really. The titles have changed but apart from that it is basically the old Roman Catholic system of professional 'Priests' running everything. We call them 'pastors' but the position is basically the same.

These are people who have gained a degree from Bible College, and now we pay them to be our "minister". Never mind the fact that we are ALL supposed to be ministers!

What this results in is two different 'classes' in the church. The "ministering" class and the "churchgoing" class (or 'laity'). Which is something that God utterly detests. He cannot stand His people being divided up into 'classes' like this. It is the doctrine of the "Nicolaitans" (Rev 2).

But is it really that bad? What harm does it really do? Below are the specific ways that this "one man pastor" model really harms the church:

1) It puts one person on a pedestal – above all others. In many churches this veneration of the pastor closely resembles Idolatry. His word is law and the entire church revolves around this one man.

2) This leads directly to PRIDE. The position that we place these men in is terribly dangerous for them and for the whole church. It is very difficult NOT to develop Pride when treated in this way. Pride is the most subtle and spiritually fatal of diseases. It wreaks havoc wherever it finds a home.

3) It turns the church into a bunch of "spectators". In other words, everybody sits around and watches while the 'professionals' do most of the work. This is an absolute disaster. For we ALL have gifts, callings and anointings from God.

4) Control, manipulation and spiritual abuse become more common where power is concentrated in the hands of one 'venerated' figure. Power corrupts, Flattery corrupts. Veneration corrupts. And before you know it, people are being terribly damaged and wounded by the control and the "management techniques" being exerted from the top. Then new teachings on "covering" and "submission" are wheeled out, to lend an air of legitimacy to the oppression that is being visited upon people. Everyone is told to 'submit' and not to question. In some denominations and churches in particular, the "one man" system lends itself to this whole scenario like a hand in a glove. Very sad.

5) The position often lends itself to "robes and titles" – or perhaps expensive 3-piece suits! Jesus said to his disciples, "You are not to be called 'Rabbi,' because you have only one Master and you are all brothers. And do not call anyone on earth 'father,' for you have one Father, and he is in heaven. Nor are you to be called 'teacher,' for you have one Teacher, the Christ." (See Matt 23:5-12, NIV). None of this seems to stop men from taking on "titles" today – and this is not just restricted to pastors, either!

6) Because the position of Pastor is usually the "only job going" in the church, it forces many who are actually evangelists or prophets to become Pastors, just so they can get to minister.

Often they are quite out of place, and many times this leads to disaster.

7) All of this creates such a load on the shoulders of the man that is appointed Senior Pastor, that this job has one of the worst BURNOUT rates in the western world.

Some people say that having a 'board of elders' who can hire or fire the pastor keeps all of this in check. Not so. It may keep the "control" side of things down, but the mere fact that they feel the need to "appoint a pastor" just shows how hooked into this system they really are. It is centuries old, and all we are doing is perpetuating it.

So how did they do things in the New Testament?

Well, the first thing we need to realize is that the original apostles were not trained "professionals". Apart from Paul they had never been to Bible College (which were run by the Chief Priests and Pharisees!) Most of the apostles were simple fishermen and tax-collectors. But they had spent MUCH TIME WITH JESUS. That was their qualification.

And it is clear that Pastors were never in charge of the church. It was the APOSTLES who were given that role. But they never "lorded it over" the people. And wherever they went they appointed elders or overseers (plural) to watch over the church in their absence. It was these 'elders' who had the "shepherding" role. Unfortunately, some Bible translations call elders "Bishops", which gives the impression of a 'hierarchy'. But this was not in the original. As Greek scholar W.E. Vine states: *"'Presbuteros', an elder, is another term for the same person as bishop or overseer. See Acts 20:17 with verse 28."* So they were just simple "elders" – that's all. It was only when the church fell into serious decline and then into Romanism that the complicated "hierarchies" began. Before this, it was all very simple. Perhaps one day it will be so again?

I am convinced that in the coming move of God the 'shepherding' role will revert to the ELDERS, just like in the early church, and the position of "Senior Pastor" that we have today will basically be abandoned as a totally unscriptural concept. The Clergy/Laity divide simply has to go.

FURTHER BIBLE STUDY:

Eph 2:19-21, Eph 4:11, 1 Cor 12:27-31, Acts 20:17, 28; Acts 14:23, Titus 1:5-9, 1 Peter 5:1-4, Matt 23:5-12, 1 Tim 3:1-9, 1 Tim 5:17, Acts 6:1-6, 1 Tim 3:10-13, Acts 2:42, Acts 13:1-3, Acts 15:1-2, Acts 16:4, Rom 16:7, 2 Cor 11:13, Rev 2:2.

CHAPTER SIX

"ENFORCED" TITHING

When I speak about "Tithing" I am not just talking about 'Giving'. Giving in itself is a wonderful thing – especially if it is from the heart. I am not against that at all. But what I am particularly addressing here is the "enforced" Tithing that is so often preached in churches today. The word "tithe" literally means 'a tenth'. And today it is used as a Law in many churches to force Christians to give one tenth of their income to that church. Many are told that they are "robbing God" if they do not give at least this much to the institution they attend each Sunday.

But is Tithing a New Testament practice at all? Is it really for Christians, or is it part of the Old Covenant? Is there really a law in force stating that all Christians must give ten percent? Or are we supposed to be "cheerful givers" – simply giving whatever God has placed on our hearts?

You may be surprised to learn how little the word 'Tithing' is even mentioned in the New Testament. In fact, there is no actual Scripture telling CHRISTIANS to tithe at all. There is one NT Scripture telling PHARISEES to tithe. But in all the letters of the apostles to the church, they never say that this was for Christians. And in the entire book of Acts (a history of the first 30 years of the Early Church) there is NOT EVEN ONE mention of tithing. There are plenty of examples of people giving money "from the heart", but NO MENTION of tithing. Isn't that interesting?

Yet people will often quote the words of Jesus to the Pharisees as though this tells CHRISTIANS to keep tithing. But it doesn't. Here is what Jesus said: "Woe to you, teachers of the law and Pharisees, you hypocrites! You give a tenth of your spices - mint, dill and cummin. But you have neglected the more important matters of the law – justice, mercy and faithfulness. You should have practiced the latter without neglecting the former." (Matt 23:23, NIV).

Notice that Jesus refers to these things as "matters of the law". That is what they are. They are matters of the Old Testament Law – not part of the New Covenant for Christians. Jesus Himself referred to them that way. And notice who he was talking to in the above passage. He was talking to LAW-KEEPING JEWS who were still under the OLD COVENANT. (The New Covenant would not begin until Jesus died and rose again). So what Jesus was saying was right – FOR THEM; but not for us – and not for now.

Yet the Tithing proponents seize on the phrase: "You should have practiced the latter without neglecting the former." The reason they seize on this is because it is the ONLY Scripture they have in the whole New Testament that even vaguely pushes Tithing! And yet it is talking to Pharisees! And it clearly states that Tithing is a "matter of the law".

The New Testament clearly teaches: "You are not under law, but under grace" (Rom 6:14). "But if you are led by the Spirit you are not under law" (Gal 5:18). In fact, the only other passage that really focuses on Tithing in the New Testament underlines this very point. At the start of Hebrews 7 there is a passage referring to tithing in the Old Testament. It clearly states that tithing is part of the Old Law (v 5). And then it goes on to say: "The former regulation is set aside because it is weak and useless (for the law made nothing perfect), and a better hope is introduced, by which we draw near to God." (Heb 7:18-19).

The point being made here is that the Old Covenant was a covenant of "regulations" (like HAVING to give one tenth) but the New Covenant is a covenant of the HEART. And we are to give out of a heart overflowing with the love of God. NOT because we are "forced" to give one tenth! The Old Law is gone. We live under a New Covenant today.

At this point, the Tithing people usually take on a different argement – that "Tithing came before the Law." They use the example of Abraham and Melchizedek (Gen 14:18-20). Therefore, they say, it still applies to us today.

Well, I have one simple question here: Isn't it true that CIRCUMCISION came before the Law also (See Gen 17)? And everyone knows that Circumcision is treated as part of the Old Law that has been done away with. It is the same with Tithing.

As former pastor Bruce Lengeman states in his article 'The Raping of the Tithe': *"The title sounds harsh, but I believe it is fairly accurate due to the damage done by the erroneous teaching of the doctrine of tithing... Plain and simple, the doctrine of tithing as it is commonly taught in the contemporary evangelical, or Bible-believing church is twisted exegesis!"*

HOW THEN SHOULD WE GIVE?

Today when it comes to 'Giving' we are often preached-to out of Malachi 3 in the Old Testament, which tells the Jewish people to "bring the full tithes into the storehouse" and says that they were "robbing God" and they were "cursed" if they did not do so (Mal 3:8-10).

Many preachers love to equate the 'storehouse' with their own church (!!), so that they can apply this Scripture to themselves. But the reality is very different. As Bruce Lengeman states: *"The 'storehouse' of Malachi has no likeness to the church structure of today. The storehouse was neither a place of assembly, nor a place of worship. It was merely a storehouse for tithed goods to be distributed to Levites, who had no inheritance, and also to widows, strangers, and orphans."*

And when we get to the Book of Acts we find that indeed MOST OF THE MONEY that came in actually went to feed and clothe the poor and the widows. In fact, it was a common practice for the Christians to sell any spare possessions and lay the money at the apostles' feet, for distribution to the poor (See Acts 4:32-37). What love these people demonstrated! And this was true giving "from the HEART", not from some "LAW" that told them how much to give.

There is also plenty of support in the New Testament for giving to those who minister the gospel (See 1 Cor 9:13-14, 1 Tim 5:17, etc.). But there is a far greater emphasis on giving to widows and orphans.

What I believe God would have us do today is be led by the Holy Spirit in our giving. Find ways to give to the poor and the widows in an effective way. (For instance, some Christian charities like 'Open Doors' support persecuted Christian widows in Islamic countries, etc). Also find effective Christian ministries to give to. We need to be free to give where God leads us – with a truly cheerful heart. As one of my readers wrote to me recently:

"You sent an email about 2 months ago that convicted me that giving was to be based on the New Testament model – giving cheerfully as we purpose – Instead of being under the law. Christ redeemed us from the curse of the law. I have found that since I give cheerfully whenever Father shows me to give that I have had my socks blessed off. I was always giving 10% to my local church and never seeing any great results. I became convicted that my worship leader needed the money so out of a strong conviction to give it to him I did so. I found that suddenly at work my sales went through the roof. Before I was doing so poorly I was close to losing my job. I know the only difference is following the Holy Spirit and doing what He tells me with my money based on the New Testament example."

C.H. wrote:

Its no joke being told to tithe on a benefit raising 3 children with no support from your ex-husband and little support from my family (my mother is a widow). Yet every church I went to laid this impossible burden on me except the Anglican church... But the guilt and condemnation laid upon me by the previous churches led me to falsely believe the reason why I was always

- 48 -

so poor was because I wasn't tithing 10% and that I had robbed God by my previous disobedience and that I needed to make it up.

All the testimonies of miraculous provision and my lack of them always kept me bound into believing that 1) It was my lack of faith, 2) I wasn't being obedient to the law of tithing, 3) I was under a curse. Try telling your hungry children why the church was getting our money and they were always going without. This went on for years. It wasn't until I stopped going to church over a year ago that I prayed and asked God to show me where to give and how much and he showed me Tear Fund Microenterprise Trust which lends money to poor people (usually widows) to get them started into business, etc, and they pay it back and someone else borrows it. And its not 10% I give but I can give freely and cheerfully to those who really need it. I feel the tithe I gave was a curse indeed – but to me for being under the Law... It never really produced fruit except occasionally the church would pay for my children to attend a camp. The provision I have needed over the years for my children was poured into church salaries and buildings and while they all lived in comfort we went without. 10% isn't much when you earn $1000 a week but it is the difference between buying food or paying a bill when you get $450 to feed, house and clothe 4 people.

Occasionally some kind folk would secretly slip me some money, but generally I was treated like an inferior (it was obvious God wasn't blessing me their way so I must be at fault). This caused me to feel such shame that I stopped mentioning my financial needs. I just got into debt on a credit card as this was the only way to make up for all the shortfall of my pay. This whole matter stinks if you ask me. Often I felt like asking the church leaders if they would like to 'live in faith' weekly for their provision for their churches like I had to for my family.

FURTHER BIBLE STUDY:

Deut 14:22-29, Matt 23:23, Rom 6:14, Gal 5:18, Heb 7:5, Heb 7:18-19, Gen 14:18-20, Gen 17:9-11, Gen 2:3, Col 2:13-14, Col 2:16-17, Rom 14:5-6, Gal 5:2-4, Acts 15:22-29, Acts 4:32-37, 1 Cor 9:13-14.

CHAPTER SEVEN

PROSPERITY AND "SEED FAITH"

A lot of people think that today's "Prosperity" teaching only affects those in the 'Word-Faith' movement. But its effects are felt far more widely than that. Jesus said, "A little leaven leavens the whole lump" and we find that this insidious teaching has infected large sections of the body of Christ in all kinds of ways. Especially in America. One of the main reasons for this is because it has aligned itself so successfully with CHRISTIAN TELEVISION.

The fact is, Christian TV can be costly, so it helps to have lots of money. And the "Prosperity" teaching is a proven money-maker for preachers. It really gets people giving! And so these kinds of preachers thrive on television. But it sure is a sick kind of "Christianity" that is presented – And quite unscriptural, as we shall see.

The Prosperity gospel basically teaches that not only does Jesus want to take away your sins and heal your body, but He also wants you to be prosperous and even "rich". Not just 'SPIRITUALLY' rich, but actually blessed with all kinds of possessions, cars and houses, etc. Because, of course, any kind of poverty and suffering is a "curse", and we know that Jesus came to set us free from the 'curse'.

Now of course there is some truth in this. If there wasn't, then this false teaching would never get off the ground. But the Bible makes it very clear that Jesus' followers can expect to SHARE IN HIS SUFFERINGS (Rom 8:17, Lk 14:27, etc). The Scriptures also speak again and again of Jesus' affinity with the POOR and His opposition to those who are rich. In fact, the sheer weight of Scriptures on this subject is staggering. It is amazing to me that the Prosperity teachers can get away with the things that they say.

There is basically only ONE verse that mentions "Prosperity" in the whole New Testament (and it is of dubious help, as we shall see). And there are dozens and dozens of verses in opposition! The only translation that really helps the Prosperity cause is the King James version: "I wish above all things that thou mayest prosper and be in health, even as thy soul prospereth" (3 John 2). Now, it is interesting to note what this word "prosper" really means in this verse. Renowned Greek scholar W.E. Vine says that it simply speaks of "the prosperity of physical and spiritual health." So it's not about MONEY at all!

And thus we find that in all the later translations, this meaning is made clear. For example, the NIV translation says: "I pray that you may enjoy good health and that all may go well with you, even as your soul is getting along well" (3 John 2). Isn't that interesting?

As I said, this is one of the only verses that these Prosperity teachers are able to use in the entire New Testament. If they are honest, they will admit that most of the rest of the NT is squarely against them.

What I would encourage anyone to do, who wants to research this subject, is to get a Concordance and look up every verse in the New Testament that contains these words: 1) Rich or Riches, 2) Money, 3) Poor, 4) Mammon, 5) Possessions, 6) Treasure, 7) Sell or Sold, etc.

You will be absolutely amazed at how strong the NT Scriptures are on this subject. I did this exact search years ago, and was astonished at what I found.

When you look up the word 'Rich' you find Scriptures such as this: "Woe unto you that are rich! For you have received your consolation" (Lk 6:24) and "How hard it is for the rich to enter the kingdom of God! It is easier for a camel to go through the eye of a needle than for a rich man to enter the kingdom of God" (Lk 18:24-25, NIV) and "People who want to GET RICH fall into temptation and a trap" (1 Tim 6:9) and "You rich people, weep and wail because of the misery that is coming upon you" (Ja 5:1). There are many more along similar lines. Go and look them up, and you will see!

We find that when Jesus was preaching kingdom principles he was very strong in this area. When the 'Rich young man' came to him, He told him: "SELL your possessions and give to the POOR, and you will have treasure in heaven. Then come, follow me" (Mt 19:21, NIV). He also told his own disciples to "SELL your possessions and give to the POOR" (Lk 12:33).

In our previous chapter on "Tithing" we discussed the whole issue of 'Giving' in the New Testament. As we saw, there is no "law" telling Christians to give 10%. In fact, what the NT makes clear is that EVERYTHING we have literally belongs to God. Many people claim that "All I have is God's" but they do not act like it! In the New Testament it is clear that it was EXPECTED for Christians to sell any spare possessions, land or houses, to give to their needy brothers and sisters – especially widows and orphans. They certainly weren't giving their money to wealthy preachers on TV! And neither were they giving it to erect a new church building on the corner! (Such things did not exist). They were giving from their HEART – and while some of it went to support the ministry, MOST of it clearly went to feed and clothe the POOR (See Acts 2:44-45, Acts 4:34-37).

Some people today want to go back to the Old Testament and use people like Solomon and Abraham as examples of RICH people to emulate. But what they fail to realize is that the Old Testament is a 'type' or a "SHADOW" of the New (Col 2:16, Heb 10:1). The Old was a "physical" covenant, with a "physical" temple and rituals, etc. The "blessings" of God were also mostly PHYSICAL and material. But today we have a "spiritual" covenant – a "heart-based" covenant, with mostly SPIRITUAL blessings. That is why we should not seek Old Testament wealth today. We live under a different covenant.

It is very obvious from the New Testament that there is NO SUCH THING as a 'Prosperity' gospel. In fact, it is the exact OPPOSITE. Jesus said, "Blessed are you who are POOR, for yours is the kingdom of God" (Lk 6:20). And James declared: "Has not God chosen those who are POOR in the eyes of the world to be rich in faith and to inherit the kingdom he promised those who love him?" (Jas 2:5, NIV). Jesus clearly stated that you "CANNOT serve God and Mammon" (Mt 6:24) and yet it is obvious that many Christians today are trying to serve BOTH. The 'Prosperity' teaching clearly encourages this. It is a very dangerous and harmful fallacy.

So does God want to bless His children or not? Of course He does! But He wants to bless us so that we can GIVE MORE AWAY – NOT so that we can hoard more luxuries to ourselves. How can it be right for some Christians to be wealthy and rolling in money and possessions, while just down the street there are Christians who barely have enough to eat? And what about our needy brothers and sisters overseas?

There is a prophecy about the coming move of God that one thing it will be built on is "Extravagant giving to the poor." I truly believe this. I am convinced that it is something very high on God's agenda.

"SEED-FAITH"

It is important that I make a few comments about the 'Seed-Faith' teaching here, because so many TV preachers use it to pressure people to give to their ministry. What it amounts to is a "Give-to-Get" doctrine that blatantly twists Scripture. When a preacher says something like, "Sow a seed of $100 into my ministry today, and God will give you back 100-fold," then they are operating out of this "Seed-Faith" doctrine. What they are really saying is, "Give to get". The motivation for giving is not so much to bless that ministry, but to GET SOMETHING BACK from God. The motivation is all twisted. Do they really expect God to "bless" something so wrong-hearted?

But certain preachers love this doctrine, because it enables them to gather huge sums of money. And surprisingly, studies have shown that it is the poor and needy who give most often to these TV preachers. Why is this? Because these people often feel that only a financial "miracle" can save them. It is not uncommon for desperate Christians to give and give, well beyond their means, in the hope that God will rescue them. Some will even lose their homes. And the elderly and the sick often give sacrificially in the hope of some kind of improvement.

Many preachers are fully aware of the kind of people they are exploiting. How sick it all is. As Jesus said in Mt 23:14, "Woe to you, scribes and Pharisees, hypocrites! For you devour widows' houses." I shudder to think of the fate that awaits some of these preachers on Judgement Day.

Much of the reasoning behind this "Seed-Faith" teaching is a distortion of 'Sowing and Reaping', which is a biblical concept. But when it is distorted by preachers and sold as a means of "Giving to get" then it has gone well beyond the Scriptures. The purity of simply "giving from the heart" is lost and replaced with selfish motives. People give because the preacher "guarantees" they will get a 'big return' on their investment! The motivation is so wrong that it is no wonder that this doctrine has produced disastrous fruit in the church. It really is one of the sickest things around.

So next time you hear a preacher using this kind of manipulation to get you to give him $100, make sure you rebuke the deception in the name of Jesus, and turn the television off!

We would all be far better to give to the POOR, as Christ commanded.

IS IT "WRONG" TO USE TELEVISION?

The obvious answer to this question is "No" – even though it is being so misused by many preachers. The fact is, Television is simply a communications medium and it can be used for either good or evil. I myself made a five-part Christian TV show for secular television a few years back in New Zealand. We made it very cheaply and interviewed ex-gang members who had become Christians, etc. So I have no problem with the medium itself. It can be very effective. The only crucial question is HOW we are using it, how much MONEY we are wasting (if any) and whether we are presenting the pure and undefiled word of the Lord. It really DOES MATTER what kind of representation of 'JESUS' we are presenting to the world. This is the big problem with much Christian television today. It is actually bringing disgrace to the name of Christ. And God will not stand for it.

I was interested to receive the following email from someone who has had recent experience with Christian TV in America. Quite a refreshing letter:

> *"I did want to comment on Christian TV. I recently left a small church that has a TV show called Crossfire. It's dedicated to youth and it is aired on Sky Angel. My husband was one of the pastors there and because of that I found out that when a ministry airs on Sky Angel, it costs them nothing. Of course there is the initial cost of cameras and editing equipment, it can be a bit pricey, and the local television stations do require certain types of video tapes – they too are costly for a small church group. However, I've often wondered after those initial costs where the millions go in some of these large well-known ministries."*

So it does not necessarily cost a fortune to get something on TV in America!

I believe that in future years we will find that God is going to use ALL of the different media to spread His message and news of the great Awakening. In the first Great Reformation, the printing press had just been invented and God used it greatly. The same is true of the Internet, Radio and even Television today. I have no problem with using these things. But it is the "WAY" that they are used that is the crucial factor. And the importance of not having them centred around 'MONEY'. I'm sure that most of you agree.

REPLIES FROM READERS:

Jeff L. wrote:

Sometime during 2003 I received an email from a Nigerian Pastor, asking for prayer. He was at a loss as to what to tell his flock who were "exhorted" (that should be extorted) by a travelling American evangelist to give money to God (to him of course) and that God would return the amount 100 fold. Of course all the flock were in that poor and needy bracket and they gave believing that God would meet their financial needs.

So the Evangelist departs with all the money and the poor Pastor is left to explain to God's people why God has not honoured their giving. They gave their food money and rent money believing God would replace it – the result was hungry, homeless people, more misery created by man in God's name. My only advice was never never never never allow these guys anywhere near your people and to teach that our giving should not be to create a debt with God.

B.E. wrote:

I want to say in response to this that my husband and I fell for this message... hook, line and sinker. We are now in such a financial mess, only God can rescue us! We once gave $1000.00 for a TV minister's airplane that we really needed for our own bills. We were told by him how anointed he was and that we were guaranteed the help we need if we help buy his airplane for ministry. Well, needless to say no help came. We have had more financial problems in the past four years because of our blindness... our willingness to accept this as the truth. God woke us up a year ago after falling on our faces and repenting. We are still in a huge struggle and hope to not go bankrupt. We have credit card debt that is insurmountable. We are told by these men, if it isn't working we are the ones at fault... we aren't giving enough... or we have sin in our lives....

"our cloud is not full enough" so we need to give more so that *"once it is filled up it will rain"*.

The Lord has kept us from drowning, and like I said before, our only hope is in Him. God help us and save us from this mess we ourselves have created.

FURTHER BIBLE STUDY:

Rom 8:17, Lk 14:27, 1 Cor 4:8-13, 3 John 2, 2 Cor 9:6-15, Matt 19:27-30, Lk 6:20-25, Lk 18:24-25, 1 Tim 6:5-10, Ja 5:1-5, Mt 19:21-24, Lk 12:33, Acts 2:44-45, Acts 4:34-37, Acts 5:1-11, James 2:2-7, Mt 6:19-24, Luke 16:19-25, Matt 13:22, Luke 19:1-10, 1 Cor 16:1-3.

CHAPTER EIGHT

IS OUR "RELIGIOUS SYSTEM" KILLING PEOPLE?

Lately I have been taking a long, hard look at the state of the Western church, and how bad things have really become. And I have come to the sad conclusion that today's religious system really is "killing" people. It is the 'system' itself that is doing this. It is set up in such a way that it is actually PREVENTING millions of people from coming into the kingdom. And thus, couldn't it be said that it is actually sending MILLIONS to hell?

I know that is a radical thing to say. But isn't it a fair conclusion to come to, at the end of the day? There are well over 100 million people attending 'church' every week in America. But how many of them are actually walking in the kingdom? How many are walking in true salvation? Or how many are headed for HELL because they are locked in a system in which they are never taught the BASIC ESSENTIALS of New Testament Christianity?

The religious system is imprisoning and destroying millions of people. It is a conclusion I had to reach. Most of them do not even have the BASIC GOSPEL preached to them anymore. If the original apostles heard what passes for the "gospel" today they would be horrified. I am convinced that there are millions upon millions of totally UNSAVED people sitting in our churches every week. And most of them are beyond our reach. They are locked away in systems in which they will NEVER hear the truth.

I have to admit that even the Pentecostal/ Charismatic system (which is my own background) is pretty much as bad as the others. In some areas it is worse. Multitudes of people are being told they are "OK" when clearly they are not. They are being fed candy-coated half-truths. How many are truly right with God or have a deep walk with Him? Isn't it true that many are not "saved" at all?

It is clear to me that we need to wage a "war" on their behalf. Not a war against people, but a war against the 'lies' that imprison them. "We do not war against flesh and blood". So it is not 'people' that we are fighting. It is the lies and deceptions that need to be brought down. The Truth will set them free.

We need to see people repent deeply from sin. We need to see the 'fear of the Lord'. We need to see good foundations laid in people's lives. And then we need to see liberty and a deep walk of communion and intimacy with God. We need to see full New Testament Christianity. "Romans 8" Christianity, where people walk before God with "no knowledge of present sin" – a totally clean conscience before Him. And when these people gather and fellowship it is truly the 'Body of Christ'. The "Religious System" is in the way of all of this – even today's "Full Gospel" Religion quite often. It is keeping people sated with half-truths and a kind of "half-Christianity". A "go to church on Sunday and you'll be alright" mentality. It really has to go. And so it is time for war. It is time to contend for these people with every ounce of Truth that we possess. It is time to smash down the lies and bring God's people out into the light. Religion is killing them. "Let my people go".

The term "Protest Movement" has been coming to my mind again and again lately, as I have been pondering what I feel God is about to do. It is interesting to note that during the Great Reformation, those who sided with the new move of God became known as "Protestants". Which was appropriate, because what Luther nailed onto the door in Wittemburg was essentially "95 Protests" at the state of the church and the things it was promoting. There was even a money-making scheme sponsored by the Pope in his day where people could "buy their relatives out of purgatory" by giving large sums of money. This was the thing that finally tipped Martin Luther over the edge. It made him sick to his stomach. And so the 'protest' began.

Years ago a friend of mine told me about a dream or vision he'd had that he felt was related to the coming move of God. In it he saw a group of "protestors" with placards and signs, marching around shouting slogans, etc. He suddenly realized that these people were protesting the STATE OF THE CHURCH. And it was not like these were "rebels" or anything. These were servants of God and this was something that God was behind. They were loudly "PROTESTING" the state of the church – for all to hear. It was quite remarkable.

I am convinced that there is a new 'Prophetic' arising that has this air of "PROTEST" about it. This movement will be blunt and direct and VERY LOUD. It will have a cause to fight for and it will make a "LOUD NOISE" about it. Its cause will be to see the church of the Living God become what she is meant to be, instead of this sickly thing that she has been. To decry the compromise and corruption we see on every hand.

For I believe that God Himself "PROTESTS" the state of today's church. He cannot stand to have her in the condition she is in. For our God cannot live with a lukewarm church.

Even a lot of people in today's 'Prophetic' movement do not seem to realize what I believe is clearly the prophet's role in seeing "Great Change" begin. Here is what I clearly understand from God: The great "SHAKING" of the church will come when the true prophets arise and SPEAK THE WORD OF THE LORD. It is critically important that they open their mouths and SPEAK a piercing word – the full 100% word of the Lord, holding nothing back. It is this act in itself that I believe will begin the tremendous "SHAKING" that has been prophesied. Let the Elijahs of God arise. Let the repentance prophets come forth. Let the "protest movement" begin.

WHO WILL DECRY THE SICKNESS?

I read a well-researched article recently about the number of private JET-PLANES that many of the top preachers and ministries in America own. Some of them cost $3500 per day just to maintain. And they cost millions of dollars to buy in the first place. Many of these people live in lavish luxury – paid for by offerings (often sent in by sick people and widows who watch their TV shows).

Now, all the time we are told "not to judge" these ministries. 'Touch not the Lord's anointed,' they say. And most of us do as we are told. We sit silently and allow it all to happen because it would be "judgemental" and 'unloving' of us to speak up about it. BUT WHAT ABOUT GOD?? What about the fact that God is mocked and publicly put to scorn by these preachers' lifestyles? What about the fact that it sets a TERRIBLE EXAMPLE for the whole church?

I believe the time has come to "PROTEST" – loud and long. This "leaven" is leavening the whole lump. It is infecting everything. I do not believe any of the leaders in the New Testament would allow such things to go unchallenged. They would speak up – even at the cost of their lives and ministries. And we have to do the same. It is time for this "PROTEST" to begin – I am convinced of it. We cannot allow these people to dishonor God in such a blatant way. It is sick, and it is affecting us all, whether we like it or not.

Let the voice of the prophets arise. Let the thunderings of God be heard. He is coming to "clean house". Let all that is counterfeit tremble. The flag of PROTEST must be raised – and it must be raised quickly.

THE HOUR FOR WAR

I am becoming more and more convinced that we are in an hour of MOBILISATION and aggressive battle. We are not to sit back and "let everything happen". We are to beat our pruning-hooks into spears and our plough-shares into swords (the 'sword of the Lord') and we are to take the fight to the enemy like never before. The Scripture tells us that "From the days of John the Baptist until now, the kingdom of heaven suffers violence, and the VIOLENT take it by force." So are YOU "violent", my friends? Or are you passive and nullified by a kind of 'fatalism' that declares "Whatever will be will be"? That is not true Christianity. True Christianity has always been WAR and battle and the clash of armies. So are you "violent" or not? Only the VIOLENT will take the kingdom in this hour. God has spoken this for years.

There are some reading this who have been "waiting" for so long that to get out of their "peace-time" mode would take a lightning bolt and a "shaking" far beyond what is healthy. I find it sad that it is not just the CHURCHES that need a good "shake" but some of us so-called 'Revival' types as well! There are some here who are about as "violent" as marshmallows. It is high time for that to change.

To those who say that we should still be in "waiting" mode, I pose this simple question: When does the 'wait' end? When entire generations have been lost? When millions upon millions sitting in our churches are eternally ruined? When the gays and transvestites and New Agers have so taken over that they possess the very gates of our cities? Is the devil to "take the youngest" forever?

I love the Scripture from the story of David and Goliath that says, "And David spoke to the men that stood near him, saying, 'What shall be done to the man who kills this Philistine and takes away the reproach from Israel? For who is this uncircumcised Philistine, that he should defy the armies of the Living God?'" (1 Sam 17:26). And the record tells us that with no armour and with 5 smooth stones as his only weapon, David RAN FULL-TILT towards that Philistine, to see His God avenged and his people's reproach removed.

We hear a lot about people with "a heart like David" in these last days. Let me tell you – David was a man of WAR. A man of 'violence'. A man of action. He would not put up with His God being put to an open shame. I wonder where the Lord will find His "Davids" today?

We live in one of the darkest hours in the history of our planet. "As it was in the days of Noah and Lot" declares the Scripture, and so it rapidly becomes. So where is the light shining in this darkness? Is it you? Is it me? Or do we slumber on? Some of us have been "waiting" for 20 years for the 'right time' (me included). Are we never to act at all? Do we just "float" on, excusing our lack of urgency and burden with the trite reply that we are "waiting on the Lord"? Will such feeble reasonings ever find a hearing in the courts of God?

There is a battle raging. It has never ceased. It is the battle for the hearts and souls of men. Let the "spectators" and idle onlookers clear the field. Let those without courage or urgency or burden retire from the scene. It is time for God's "mighty men of valor" to come forth. The hour is late and the time will soon arrive when no man can work. "In season and out of season" said Paul, and it is time for us to heed his words. If ever there was an hour for the "Gideon's 300" it is now.

Years ago God spoke these words to me: "WHO DARES WINS". It is not enough to simply pray. For many have prayed and yet not taken the kingdom. And neither is it enough to prophesy. For many have brought endless "words" and yet the kingdom remains undisturbed. The phrase "Who DARES Wins" is the motto of the British SAS – men of action who operate behind enemy lines and who revel in courage and fighting spirit. So it will be with this great end-times Army of God.

If you don't have the stomach for it, hang back and do nothing. Nobody will notice. But let the mighty ones of God arise in this hour. Let those who have been prepared of God in the caves and the deserts come forth. You have awaited a trumpet blast. Do you not hear it? Gird up your loins, you mighty men. Prepare for war. Let the armies of the enemy tremble. Arm of the Living God, put on strength! The Lord of Hosts is about to arise and scatter His enemies. Can you not scent the blood in the air?

CHAPTER NINE

BIBLE COLLEGES

You know, a lot of people questioned my motives for publishing this series on "The Nine Lies of Today's church". They asked, "Why should a Revival and Repentance preacher like you get embroiled in such 'OUTWARD' matters? After all, many of these issues are not really "Heart" issues at all. Things like the 'One-man Pastor' system and "Church Buildings" seem like such EXTERNAL matters. (And this issue of 'Bible Colleges' is not much different). So why bother with them?"

Well, the thing I have noticed about these old traditions (which we have treated as "normal" for years), is that they all add to the little "prison" that we have built for ourselves in the church today. In their own way, each of them builds a little "wall" of untruth around itself, and when you add them all together you have a virtual "prison" of untruths that is holding us back from being what we are meant to be. The TRUTH sets us free, remember. And we are a long way from the Book of Acts today – partly because of this great 'wall' of traditions that we adhere to.

Of course, personal Revival and deep repentance and deep seeking of God are the most important things. These are the real 'Heart' issues. But it is a fact that God will need a "new wineskin" after His 'new wine' is poured out. And we need to know what belongs to the "Old" and why we need to leave it behind, or we are bound to try and include it in the "New". Then our children will have to have another Reformation to correct what we have left undone. Do you see what I am saying?

The coming move of God will be a REFORMATION as well as a Revival. There will be a new wineskin. So we must be aware of the things we need to leave behind. These little "walls" have got to go.

The church has to break out of this 'prison' of 1700-year-old traditions if it is ever to look like the early church again. And yes, some of this does involve "outward" things. BIBLE COLLEGE is a good example. The fact is the early church had no such thing. And they had more power with God than any group of people that has ever lived. There is simply NOTHING LIKE a Bible College in the Book of Acts, and you would have to conclude that they were better off without it! More miracles, more anointing, more prayer, more depth of communion with God. So who needs a Bible College?

As we have already discussed, the early apostles were mostly not "educated" men at all. They were fishermen and tax collectors! It was the Scribes and Pharisees who were the learned Bible-scholars of their day. These were the "professional clergy" of that time. "And when they saw the boldness of Peter and John, and perceived that they were UNLEARNED and IGNORANT men, they marveled; and they took knowledge of them, that they had BEEN WITH JESUS" (Acts 4:13).

So there it is, in black and white. These apostles were "unlearned and ignorant" in the eyes of the religious leaders of their day. But because they had BEEN WITH JESUS they would shake the world.

But what damage do Bible Colleges and Seminaries actually do? Are they really that harmful? There are several ways in which they do great harm. Think about these points for a moment:

1. Bible Colleges are the linchpin of the false divide between the "clergy" and the "laity" (which God hates). In other words, this is where the doctrine of the "Priesthood of ALL believers" is trodden underfoot by the church. As soon as you have certain people who go away to a University or College to become "qualified" professional ministers, then you have lost New Testament Christianity. These people are allowed to 'minister' because they have a Bible College degree or diploma, while other people aren't, because they do not have the 'piece of

paper'. It does not matter what their gifts or callings may be. Often the church will put people on a shelf if they do not have the right academic "qualification". They may get to minister in a limited way, but in most cases this is quite restricted.

Now, don't you think this is SICK? What on earth would 'unlearned' fishermen like Peter and John do in such a world? Would they even pass the entrance exams? Naturally, they would NEVER be allowed to lead the church without a Bible College degree today! The Day of Pentecost would have to wait until they got themselves properly "qualified".

As I said, the Bible College is the 'linchpin' of this whole set-up. It is the place where you go to become a "professional". It is the place where the "divide" happens. You go there as a mere "lay-person" and you come out as "clergy" - with all the rights and privileges which stem from that in today's world. And then the whole church is trained to sit back and let you do most of the work. The concept of the "whole Body ministering" is totally lost - mostly through this ONE ERROR.

2. Charles Finney said: *"I am still solemnly impressed with the conviction, that the schools are to a great extent spoiling* [or ruining] *the ministers."* Today we are all aware of many Bible Schools where a lot of time is spent questioning the validity and sources of many books of the Bible, questioning whether events in Scripture really happened that way, etc. Human reasoning and man's wisdom naturally tend to come to the fore in such "mind"-oriented and intellectual places. And a lot of young, zealous preachers are indeed "ruined" by attending such schools. Their head is filled with doubts and their heart quickly loses its fire. Some of them are ruined for life. But what about the so-called "good" schools? Where there is a solid belief in Scripture and many Spirit-filled tutors?

Well, the fact is, the whole CONCEPT of Bible Colleges is in error. The whole idea of having to study theories, sit exams, and gain a piece of paper that "qualifies" you for the ministry is a serious deception. And even the "good" Bible Schools are often simply churning out "systemized" men to keep the church 'machine' churning along. They are taught how to keep the system well-oiled - how to get the 'programs' running efficiently and so-on. All of this is the very opposite of the early church.

So what are the TRUE "qualifications" for ministry that we need to take heed of? Well, firstly, we must have mature spiritual gifts and a calling from God. And we need to be someone who has spent much time ALONE WITH GOD in prayer. Also, to be a leader in the church we need to fulfill the requirements of 1 Tim 3:1-13. "If anyone sets his heart on being an overseer, he desires a noble task. Now the overseer must be above reproach, the husband of but one wife, temperate, self-controlled, respectable, hospitable, able to teach, not given to drunkenness, not violent but gentle, not quarrelsome, not a lover of money. He must manage his own family well and see that his children obey him with proper respect. (If anyone does not know how to manage his own family, how can he take care of God's church?) He must not be a recent convert, or he may become conceited... He must also have a good reputation with outsiders..." The failure to stick to the above guidelines in choosing leaders in today's church has resulted in all kinds of disasters.

So is there any place for "training" in the church? Certainly! But it clearly needs to be 'PRACTICAL' training, rather than mainly academic or intellectual training. And I believe we need to avoid the whole "degrees and diplomas" syndrome altogether. There are many short-term training camps and practical courses that are very helpful for Christians. I see nothing wrong with many of these. YWAM has run "Discipleship Training Courses" for years, which I understand are 3-month practical discipleship courses ending with a missions trip to minister to the poor and needy, etc. A lot of these kinds of things are excellent. But NOTHING can take the place of simply spending MUCH TIME alone with God. This is the major qualification that the early apostles had, after all. And it should be no different today.

It is also possible to find the occasional Bible School that is deeply spiritual and practical. Often these are small and little-known. Charles Finney himself became a tutor at a new Bible School called 'Oberlin College' in the 1830's. A lot of his lectures amounted to full-on "Revival" preaching! But of course, now Oberlin is far removed from being a center of Revival. And that is the problem. It is usually in the second or third generation after they are founded that most of these colleges become stale and institutionalized. And it is then that they usually start doing much more harm than good.

A number of people wrote to me asking about our domain name "www.revivalschool.com". Why did we choose such a name if we did not believe in Bible Schools? Well, we are yet to get any kind of "Online Revival School" going at all, which is what I want to do someday. But rest assured it will be a very "practical" thing aimed at teaching people the secrets of "personal" Revival and then "corporate" Revival as well. One day we will get it happening!

FURTHER BIBLE STUDY:

Matt 11:25-26, Matt 18:3, Acts 4:13, 1 Cor 1:19-29, 1 Cor 3:18-20, Matt 23:5-12, 1 Tim 3:1-13, Titus 1:5-9, 1 Peter 5:1-4,   Acts 6:1-6.

CHAPTER TEN

THE "TWO SECRETS" OF REVIVAL

The two secrets of Revival that we are about to look at, have very little to do with the "structural" problems of the church that we have been discussing. In fact, they are probably far more important in a lot of ways.

If people have these two things happening, then there is little else that I care about. It doesn't bother me if they have a "church building" program and a Bible College and every other thing. If they have these two things happening then these other issues pale by comparison. We need to realize that changing many of the 'outward' things that we have been discussing would achieve very little in itself. It is like re-arranging the "boxes" or the outward shell. It is like trying to form a new wineskin but forgetting about the 'new wine' that goes in it.

So it is high time that we talked about obtaining this NEW WINE from God. That is what true Revival is all about.

Some of you will have read about these "2 Secrets" before. But please read this section anyway, because I am going to be applying them in a way that goes beyond what I have written in the past.

The two key questions that we will be covering in this chapter are: 1) How do I get into a state of "Personal Revival", and 2) How do we get from there into a state of "Corporate Revival"?

As many of you know, I have been studying Revival history now for many years. I have looked at Revivals from recent decades and Revivals from centuries ago. And after all this research, I have found that the secrets of Revival seem to boil down to two main things.

These things are: 1) Extremely deep REPENTANCE, and 2) A kind of "wrestling, agonizing" prayer – crying to God for the "OUTPOURING" of His Holy Spirit.

These two things have been the secrets to countless Revivals down the ages – and I fully believe they will be so again. That is why there is NOTHING more important that we need to be discussing right now.

ACTUALLY "EXPERIENCING" DEEP REPENTANCE

As Frank Bartleman (from the 'Azusa Street' Revival) wrote: "I received from God early in 1905 the following keynote to revival: 'The DEPTH of revival will be determined exactly by the DEPTH of the spirit of REPENTANCE.' And this will obtain for all people, at all times."

I can affirm that all history backs up Bartleman's words here. And I can also tell you that if you want to get into a truly "Revived" state – or a state of "personal Revival" – then DEEP Repentance is one of the keys.

What we often find is that Christians have turned away from a lot of the "obvious" sins, such as lying, stealing, adultery, etc. But there are other things that they are aware of in their lives that are not right. It is dealing with these "other things" that can be the key to a far greater intimacy with God.

Do you know that God HATES all sin, and that when you get close to God then your heart will HATE sin just like He does?

So let's get "practical" with this. Here is what you need to do to deal with these things at a DEEP level: Firstly, get off by yourself with God. You need time alone in a quiet place with Him. Secondly, ask and plead with God to "shine His light" into your heart. To show you any unclean thing, whether it be unforgiveness, lust, speaking against people behind their backs, holding grudges, little "white" lies, etc. Ask God to show you how HE FEELS about sin. Ask Him to shine His light deep inside you and show you things that you need to confess and renounce and ask forgiveness for. In some cases, you may need to go to a brother or sister and apologize to them or even make restitution. Make sure the repentance goes to the DEEPEST LEVEL possible. Confess each sin specifically to God, turn from it and ask God to cleanse you. With a lot of people it is these so-called "MINOR" SINS that are holding them back.

Here is one last quote on this subject from Evan Roberts of the Welsh Revival: "First, is there any sin in your past with which you have not honestly dealt – not confessed to God? On your knees at once. Your past must be put away and cleansed. Second, is there anything in your life that is doubtful – anything you cannot decide whether it is good or evil? Away with it. There must not be a trace of a cloud between you and God. Have you forgiven everybody – EVERYBODY? If not, don't expect forgiveness for your sins..."

This issue of TRULY forgiving those who have hurt you can be a big one. It is important to be BRUTALLY HONEST with yourself. Is there still "bad feeling" deep inside you towards certain people? Is there a trace of bitterness when you speak about that person? We all need to get before God and repent and RENOUNCE all unforgiveness from deep within us. Going through this whole "deep repentance" process is the first key to personal Revival.

"WRESTLING, AGONIZING" PRAYER:

When you study history, you soon notice that there is a specific type of prayer that you see in Revivals again and again. When I first began to study past moves of God I quickly realized this, because I came across it so often. This special type of prayer is an ESSENTIAL ingredient of Revival.

The old Revivalists used to speak of having the "spirit of prayer". They spoke of weeping, agonizing, pleading, wrestling, 'travailing' in prayer. The whole reason that these Revival preachers were so anointed and saturated with the presence of God was because they had truly broken through, right into His very throne-room in prayer, and had spent much time communing with Him there. This type of praying has always been one of the most important keys to true Revival.

Charles Finney said, "Unless I had the spirit of prayer I could do nothing... I found myself unable to preach with power and efficiency, or to win souls..." George Whitefield said: "Whole days and WEEKS have I spent prostrate on the ground in silent or vocal prayer..." Frank Bartleman wrote: "At night I could scarcely sleep for the spirit of prayer... Prayer literally consumed me." And D.M. McIntyre wrote: "Before the great revival in Gallneukirchen broke out, Martin Boos spent hours and days and often nights in lonely agonies of intercession. Afterwards, when he preached, his words were as flame, and the hearts of the people as grass."

As history shows, the church can only expect true Revival when a remnant of God's people get DESPERATE – desperate about the backslidden state of the church, desperate about the lukewarmness within them and all around them, desperate about sin and compromise, desperate about the fact that God is not GLORIFIED, that He is not truly LORD of His church, that His words are mocked and largely seen as irrelevant by a dying world. Revival will come when God's people truly humble themselves, when they replace their "positive imaging" ('Rise up, you people of power", etc), with the reality of James' lament: "Be afflicted, and mourn, and weep: let your laughter be turned to mourning, and your joy to heaviness. Humble yourselves in the sight of the Lord, and He shall lift you up" (Jas 4:9-10).

As was said of Evan Roberts: "He would break down, crying bitterly for God to bend them, in an agony of prayer, the tears coursing down his cheeks, with his whole frame writhing." And John Wesley asked: "Have you any days of fasting and prayer? Storm the throne of grace and persevere therein, and mercy will come down." Brothers, sisters, we need to get DESPERATE in our praying!

HOW TO "WRESTLE" IN PRAYER

Now, it is very important to realize that this type of prayer is not just for "special" people or leaders. It is absolutely one of the keys to "personal Revival" for every one of us. The Bible makes it very clear that the "effectual fervent prayer of a righteous man" is available to us all.

And history shows that "wrestling Revival prayer" can actually be TAUGHT to Christians. This comes through loud and clear in the book 'Anointed for Burial', which is Todd and DeAnn Burke's account of the mighty Revival in Cambodia in the 1970's. It occurred when God had already been moving there for some time. Todd wrote: "Referring to Genesis 32, I told them how Jacob WRESTLED with the Lord until He blessed him. 'If we expect power and blessing from the Lord, we are going to have to be willing to wrestle with Him in prayer and fasting, in self-denial, in taking up our cross,' I said. Then I shared with them from a devotional book by Hudson Taylor, 'An easy-going, non-self-denying life will never be one of power.' With that, everyone began to wrestle in prayer, and before long, the blessing came."

When these people broke up into prayer groups and began to "wrestle" with God in prayer as Todd had taught them, the result was actual "OUTPOURINGS" of the Holy Spirit. (i.e., The Holy Spirit descending upon whole groups of Christians just like in Acts, with incredibly powerful results). It was an amazing time.

Notice that these Christians were actually TAUGHT to "wrestle" with God in this way. And they simply went and did it! Early in the 1904 Welsh Revival, Evan Roberts taught the children of Moriah to pray this simple prayer: "Send the Spirit to Moriah for Jesus Christ's sake." Later, he developed this same concept for his general meetings. Because it was vital that people plead with God to "send His Spirit" down upon them.

After all, this is exactly what Pentecost was all about. It was the

120 in the upper room, crying out to God for ten days, and then God "sending His Spirit" like a mighty rushing wind, and filling them to overflowing. In the past 50 years, there have been many powerful Revivals in which God outpoured His Spirit in a similar way. When God "outpours" His Spirit like this, it is far more than a person simply being baptized in the Spirit. It is a general "outpouring".

In fact, an "Outpouring of the Holy Spirit" is the essence of what Revival truly is. And just like Pentecost, the result is that many become FILLED with the Holy Spirit, and many others become greatly CONVICTED of their sin. True Revival is the Glory of God coming down. It is His Spirit being "POURED OUT" in a specific place or upon a specific people. We need to 'wrestle' with God to see such an outpouring occur in our day.

Now, before you can 'wrestle' with God in prayer, here is what you need to do: 1) Become DESPERATE to see God GLORIFIED in the earth; 2) Cleanse your "hands" and your "heart" so that you can truly enter into the throne-room of God; 3) Plead with God to outpour His "spirit of prayer" upon you; 4) Nurture His "fire" in your heart, so that you can 'agonize' in prayer before Him; 5) When you do pray, be very SPECIFIC in 'wrestling' with God to outpour His Spirit upon YOURSELF or upon a specific group. We all need this fresh infilling.

If you can do these simple things, then TODAY is the day when you can begin to "wrestle" with God in prayer. Do not delay. This could be the key to seeing you transformed by "personal Revival" and coming into a far deeper communion with God.

IN SUMMARY

Having studied Revivals now for over 20 years, I am convinced that the road to "personal Revival" is really the same as the road to 'corporate Revival'. The major keys have always been "deep repentance" and 'agonizing' prayer. Our motives for seeking God must never be selfish ones. We should be seeking Him for His own sake, not for what He can "do for us". It is to see HIM GLORIFIED that we ask these things.

So, my friends, all I can do is urge you to get into a quiet place and give yourself to heart-searching repentance and "agonizing" prayer until you see a massive "BREAKTHROUGH" in your Christian walk. We all need to be filled with His Spirit again and again. Since I was 17 years old, I would attribute almost every spiritual breakthrough in my life to these two 'Revival' secrets. They have truly revolutionized my life.

So what about "Corporate" Revival – where God's Spirit is poured out upon whole communities and cities? Well, what God will often do is what He did at Pentecost. He will take His "Revived" ones and use them to bring Revival to others. In other words, if God can find a GROUP of people who have gone through "personal Revival", then He can use them to speak Truth and carry His anointing into whole areas; and to PRAY for further outpourings.

So what does God need to find in the earth today? Simply GROUPS of "Revived" Christians who can begin to preach repentance and pray for God's Spirit to be outpoured. It all starts with people who have been "Revived".

As A.T. Pierson wrote, "From the day of Pentecost, there has been not one great spiritual awakening in any land which has not begun in a union of prayer, though only among two or three; no such outward, upward movement has continued after such prayer meetings declined."

I know that the truths in this chapter actually WORK in the real world because I have experienced them myself. I pray that they will truly revolutionize many lives.

CHAPTER ELEVEN

"SUNDAY DISUNITY"

Let me ask a simple question here: Doesn't the fact that we all meet at the same time every Sunday create COMPETITION and DIVISION in the church?

Before you answer that, let us analyze what actually happens all over the world on Sunday mornings.

In the West on Sunday, most Christians get up and drive perhaps five or ten miles (maybe more) to get to their favorite church. Some attend locally but many do not. And even the 'local' attendees have to choose between several different denominations in their area.

Now, all of these buildings that we attend have different "labels" on them, and we have to choose ONE of them because they all meet at the same time. So we become "labelled" by the group that we attend. We become a "Baptist" or "Assembly of God" or "Vineyard" or "Pentecostal Holiness", etc, etc. Most of the time we never really get to know the local Christians on our street at all, because they are all going off to their own groups – and so we never really get to fellowship together. We meet with "OUR" group – and we hardly even know the Christians in our own neighborhood.

Now, does any of this sound "right" to you? Does any of this sound like the Book of Acts?

The fact is Sunday morning has turned into a time of DIVISION, where we all have to choose which 'sect' or denomination of the church we are going to attend. It is the time when we all separate ourselves into "catagories". Which church do you go to? This becomes an important question. That is, "Which DIVISION do you belong to?" 'Which hierarchy do you come under?' "Who is your covering?" 'What box can we put you in?'

The attempts at so-called "unity" in the church today are often rather feeble. They usually amount to one-off 'events', where we all gather together for a day, but afterwards go straight back to our "divided" lifestyles again. Or there may be a regular meeting of the local pastors – which is seen as a kind of "unity".

But when that meeting is over, the fact is that all of these groups are basically in COMPETITION with one another (especially the Charismatic and Pentecostal ones). They all meet at the same time each week – hoping for more members to join "THEIR" group. And they all have their own hierarchies, their own 'label', their own "stream" that they are a part of (even the so-called "Non-denominational" churches very often).

Some have likened this situation to "fast-food" chains, because the set-up is quite similar. Let us suppose that Burger King sets up a restaurant just down the street from a McDonalds. Now, the two managers may be quite friendly on the surface. They may even attend local meetings of the "Fast-Food Togetherness" club. But the fact is, they are SELLING THE SAME PRODUCT just down the street from one another. They need more customers and they are in TOTAL COMPETITION with each other. Can anybody conceive of true "unity" between Burger King and McDonalds? Not in a million years! (Not unless they buy each other out). There is NO UNITY to be had in that scenario. It is designed for COMPETITION. And the structure of the church today is virtually identical. We are all 'down the street' from our main competition – EACH OTHER. The system itself does not allow for unity. It was built out of competing 'streams', denominations and divisions. While we keep this system, there is about as much chance for TRUE unity as McDonalds becoming "one" with Burger King tomorrow.

Jesus prayed concerning His followers "that they all may be

ONE... that the world may BELIEVE." This disunity and division that is so obvious to all, is one of the huge reasons why the world does not BELIEVE what we say today. They point to our divisions and (quite rightly) disdain our words.

As we have discussed before, in the Book of Acts there was ONE church – united under the leadership of the apostles. They had huge citywide gatherings and smaller house-fellowships, but they were all ONE BODY. When they met together "from house to house" it was basically ALL the local Christians from that neighborhood. They lived and fellowshipped with one another within their own local area. THAT is what "local church" really means!

But today we cannot just be part of the "whole Body", can we? We have to choose a 'division' to belong to – otherwise we are seen as 'heretics'. I believe the original apostles would be rolling in their graves if they could see the way the church is set up today.

If only we could see ourselves through their eyes. Every Sunday we dress up and go to our Division's "cathedral", where we sit down, stand up, sing our "five fast songs and five slow songs", listen to the sermon, place our money in the offering bag, hear the notices and go home. Week-in and week-out, it is almost always the same. And we think this is "church life"!

As the early Pentecostal pioneer Frank Bartleman wrote: *"We drift back continually into the old, backslidden, ecclesiastical conceptions, forms and ceremonies. Thus history sadly ever repeats itself. Now we must work up an annual revival. We go to church on Sundays, etc, etc, just 'like the nations (churches) round about us.' But in the beginning it was not so."*

SO HOW DO WE FIND TRUE UNITY?

The answer to this question is that we have GOT to get out from under all these "LABELS". We have to abandon a religious system that simply does not allow us to BE THE CHURCH as she is meant to be. I know this sounds 'drastic', but I have been pondering this subject for years and it is very clear to me that there is NO WAY BACK to the simple unity of the early church unless we abandon our denominational divisions. Today's structure CANNOT be reformed. It is a disaster area – and 'division' is at the very heart of it.

As the renowned Christian writer John Bunyan declared: *"Since you desire to know by what name I wish to be called, I desire, if God should count me worthy, to be called a Christian, a believer, or any other name sanctioned by the Holy Ghost. But as for those factious titles, such as Anabaptists, etc, I believe they came neither from Jerusalem nor Antioch, but rather from hell and Babylon, for they naturally tend to divisions, and ye may know them by their fruits."*

But HOW do we get the whole church back to the type of unity they had in the Book of Acts? How on earth do we get people to abandon these DIVISIONS?

I am convinced that it will take a full-blown AWAKENING to do this. And I am convinced that this Awakening will result in a church that is based OUTSIDE the "four walls" – just like Acts. Why is it so important to get people out of their religious environments and walls? Because of all the "learnt behavior" and DIVISIONS that go with those surroundings. People have to leave it all behind to even see how harmful it is. And also, it is only outside that we can actually experience "one body" as a reality. When people truly experience the love and unity of gathering with fellow believers OUTSIDE THE WALLS – then they will realize what we have been missing all these years; and how simple it is. God wants us to LIVE THIS WAY all the time – not just on special occasions.

Once people have experienced what true unity is like, I believe this will naturally lead to "house to house" fellowship in their own neighborhoods. It is just a continuation of the same concept.

Now, just to be clear here: I do not believe in "dumbing down" our Christianity to achieve unity. I do not believe in uniting around the "lowest common denominator". Instead, I believe we need to RAISE our standards and unite around that. So that nothing less than a glorious, Spirit-imbued church-life will do – pure and holy, filled with the glory of God. It is not "unity at all costs" that I am preaching here. It is uniting around the TRUTH and the outpouring of the Spirit of God.

By the way, I think we need to AVOID SUNDAY MORNINGS for our meeting times! Otherwise we are simply in "competition" with the churches. Let's break away from this destructive pattern this time, shall we?

FURTHER BIBLE STUDY:

Jn 17:20-23, 1 Cor 1:10-13, Acts 1:4-5, Acts 1:8, Acts 1:13-14, Acts 2:1-4, Acts 2:42-47, Acts 5:12-16, Acts 20:7, 1 Cor 16:1-3, Acts 5:42.

CHAPTER TWELVE

NOW FOR LOVE AND SIMPLICITY

Some people may not realize, but the purpose of this "Nine Lies" series has been to clear away as much 'junk' as possible – so we can actually SEE what the early church was like.

Imagine a massive slab of rock, which is like the "foundation" that the original apostles laid in the early church. Then imagine 2000 years worth of all kinds of structures being bolted onto this foundation – brick and glass and steel of all shapes and sizes. A huge hodge-podge of structures that has taken hundreds of years to erect (A tangle of God's ideas and man's ideas all mixed together).

What we have been trying to do, in essence, is take a bunch of bulldozers and a wrecking crew and scrape this huge unwieldy tangle off the rock, so we can actually see the original "foundation" underneath – in its original pristine form.

And what do we find when we get right back to the "original" thing? We find LOVE and freedom and simplicity of the most rare and precious kind. We find a group of people without pretension – who loved God and each other with all their hearts.

You know, I have grown very weary of playing the role of "demolition man" – even though I realize it is probably necessary so we can get right down to the 'foundation' again. I have been so much looking forward to getting the 'demolition' over with, so we can take another look at the original church with new eyes. I believe it is time to do just that.

God has been speaking to me a lot lately about SIMPLICITY and LOVE. And when I look at the early church, I see this everywhere. This was not a "complicated" set-up. In fact, it was the

'ABSENCE' of complication that helped make it what it was. These people did not have to worry about church boards or Seminaries or building funds or Denominations or creeds or rituals or TV preachers or any of those things. (None of it had even been invented yet!)

They simply loved God and loved each other. And everything else flowed out of that. There was a "child-like" quality to their Christianity that we have to get back to. And if we are willing to leave the 'junk' behind, I believe we can.

You know, in all His dealings with men, what God has really been wanting to re-establish is His simple yet profound relationship with Adam in the garden. The two of them used to walk together in the "cool of the day", communing with one another like the closest of friends. And ever since then, God has wanted to see this relationship restored. And through Jesus, at last there is a way. But how many of us live in that place of deep communion with God today? Isn't it a tragedy that Jesus died so every one of us can get back to this kind of relationship with God – yet so few of us live in it?

But it is possible. In fact, this is the key to the love and simplicity of the early church. There is a key Scripture that we need to look at: "For the kingdom of God is not meat and drink; but righteousness, peace and joy in the Holy Spirit" (Rom 14:17). Notice that "righteousness" comes before 'peace and joy'. This is the key here. If our heart can become truly right before God, then these other things will naturally follow. And if we can get a GROUP of people whose hearts are right before God (who have "no consciousness" of present sin – which WALK in the washing of the blood of Jesus) then that whole group can experience the kind of unity and simplicity and love that the early church walked in. As I said, the key is "righteousness" – and then will come 'peace and joy'.

A lot of people try all kinds of things to get peace and joy in their lives – but they still cling to certain sins in their hearts (especially unforgiveness) and wonder why they never find it.

Just imagine for a moment that a group of people could be found who walked before God with a pure heart like this. And imagine if they had left all the Religious 'junk' and paraphernalia behind and simply gathered together and loved God and loved each other. It is the ABSENCE of this 'junk' that makes things simple. Imagine the love and the joy and the peace that these people could walk in if they just forgot about all that stuff and simply focused on HIM. This is what the early church was like. Jesus said: "I tell you the truth, unless you change and become like LITTLE CHILDREN, you will never enter the kingdom of heaven" (Mt 18:3, NIV).

In the 1960's, the "hippies" tried to achieve this kind of thing, but ultimately failed, because what they were doing was not built on heart-righteousness. But it is certainly possible if the righteousness of God is at the center of it. Man has a deep longing to see a people who live in true harmony and love and simplicity. This is the essence of what was lost in Eden. And we all have an inbuilt longing to return to it somehow. If people ever see the real thing, they will surely respond.

In this book we have spent a lot of time talking about what the church is NOT – and trying to remove all the 'junk'. But to become like the original church once more, we need to forget all these complications and become 'child-like' in our Christianity again. For only then can LOVE and SIMPLICITY abound.

'EDEN' AND THE KINGDOM OF GOD

There is more to say on this subject of 'Eden'. Let us begin with this question: Have you ever thought deeply about how much the original church was actually like the Garden of Eden? Seriously. When we read at the beginning of Acts what the early church was like, it so closely resembles the harmony, unity and love of the original 'paradise on earth' – it is amazing. I believe this is a very significant point to grasp.

Read this passage once again and take it deep into your soul: Acts 2:42-46 (NIV), "They devoted themselves to the apostles' teaching and to the fellowship, to the breaking of bread and to prayer. Everyone was filled with awe and many wonders and miraculous signs were done by the apostles. All the believers were together and had everything in common. Selling their possessions and goods, they gave to anyone as he had need. Every day they continued to meet together in the temple courts. They broke bread in their homes and ate together with glad and sincere hearts..."

Can you imagine being part of something like that? The simple love and unity and devotion? The lack of 'Religion'? The childlike faith? Jesus said, "By this all men will know that you are my disciples, if you LOVE one another."

We spoke earlier about how the "hippie" movement of the 1960's tried to recapture this 'paradise lost'. But they found that their hearts were not capable of entering it unless they ingested large quantities of marijuana and LSD to make themselves "loving" and peaceful. Thus it was only a temporary thing. It faded when the drugs wore off. It was not how they really were, deep inside.

As I said before, people everywhere have a deep longing for this "lost Eden" and wish that there were some way of finding it again. Sadly, they look at the church today and we seem to be no closer to it than anybody else. What a tragedy.

I am convinced that God wants us to truly live in 'Eden' today – first in our own hearts and then amongst one another. I believe this has always been His desire – to return us to our state before the fall; to walk before Him in innocence and love, with "no knowledge of present sin".

This is what the "kingdom" really is. It is any place where God's will is done "on earth as it is in heaven". In other words, when you experience the kingdom, then you experience a place "like heaven" –first inside you and then amongst one another. Jesus said, "The kingdom of heaven is at hand." Meaning that there was a visible manifestation of this kingdom about to appear before their eyes. And His words were fulfilled in the early church – which lived before the world in a kind of 'paradise' of the heart. They fully displayed His kingdom for the first time since the fall. And they did it without drugs because their heart was so right with God. Who needs drugs when the "kingdom of God is within you"?

Do you know that what we are talking about here is the 'NORMAL' state of the church? In other words, if people do not see this amongst us, then how can we claim to be the church? If we are not like the "original" then what are we doing claiming to be true Christianity? Do you realize that when we talk about 'Revival' we are simply talking about the church returning to this Edenic state – just for a time? 'Revival' seems to be the only time the church truly walks in the 'kingdom'. It is the church returning to 'normal' for awhile. And then it is lost and God has to try again to bring us back to it.

So how exactly do we get back into this state? Well, the answer is there, right at the start of Acts. That is how the early church came into it. I was reading the book "Rees Howells Intercessor" recently – about an anointed Welshman back in the early 1900's who was sent as a missionary to Gazaland, Africa. And the 'Pentecost' that occurred there just confirmed the simplicity of the whole process to me:

"They had no word in their language for revival, so he told them about Pentecost: that it was God who had come down then, moving upon the hearts of men and women... and that He would do the same with them, if they were willing to repent.... he continued to speak to them about Revival, and in six weeks the Spirit began to move upon the Christians... Mrs. Howells taught them the chorus, 'Lord, send a revival, And let it begin in me'...."

"While they were on their knees, the Lord spoke to Mr. Howells, telling him that their prayer was heard and the revival was coming... the Holy Ghost was coming down to give a Pentecost

in their district. 'In the evening down he came. I shall never forget it... within five minutes the whole congregation were on their faces crying to God. Like lightning and thunder the power came down. I had never seen this even in the Welsh Revival. I had only heard about it with Finney and others... The next day He came again, and people were on their knees till 6 p.m. This went on for six days and people began to confess their sins and come free as the Holy Spirit brought them through.'"

As the Revival spread far and wide, Rees wrote of the great joy that resulted from forgiveness and deep cleansing in these people. Truly it was "heaven come to earth". An 'Eden' had come down among them.

So now we see the secrets confirmed – very similar to our last chapter. It is really no different to Pentecost. There was 1) Intense PRAYER for an outpouring, 2) An anointed 'repentance' PREACHER, 3) A great OUTPOURING of the Holy Spirit, 4) Deep REPENTANCE leading to deep joy and forgiveness. This is how these people came into a state of truly "living in the kingdom." And as I have said before, we see this repeated again and again, right down through history.

It seems that these are the simple keys to coming into the 'Eden' experience of the early church. They have been proven time and time again. And with a 'new wineskin' it has been shown that such Revivals can last for up to forty years – not just a few. As always, they start with God's people simply crying out to Him for an "outpouring". This is something we can all do. It is that simple. So will you join me in pleading for a 'Pentecost', my friends? For that is where it all has to start.

CHAPTER THIRTEEN

PROGRAMS AND MORE PROGRAMS

The fact that today's church revolves largely around MAN and not around God is obvious to many who observe how she functions from day to day. The sad fact is, when the Holy Spirit is not moving in any great way, man is always ready and willing to step in and "help God out" by taking over the running of the church. And humans are always full of "great ideas" for expanding the work as well. Much of this activity can be excused as being "good" activity, of course. We can find every reason in the world why we should be adding new programs, activities and meetings – and keeping the Christians busy, busy, busy with church things. But the sad fact is, it is often the truly essential things that get neglected – like prayer meetings – where we might actually get in touch with GOD instead of just running around "DOING, DOING, DOING." But strangely, getting in touch with God does not seem to be very high on the agenda today. Instead it often seems to be "building up OUR church" – and all the activities related to that. Man's ideas rule and God's voice is crowded out by all the busyness and self-promotion.

When I was compiling all the emails from "Out-of-church" Christians for my book on that subject, I noticed that one of the biggest reasons that these people gave for leaving their churches was this glut of 'activity' and the LACK OF GOD. They simply could not live with this overwhelming "program-mentality" in the church. It simply reeked of MAN. It is also significant that many of these "Out-of-church" types had actually been leaders of some kind in the church. Often they had been very active for years and years. They had seen the whole thing from the inside and they wanted out. Enough of MAN. They wanted more of GOD.

So what was the Early Church like in this regard? What kind of programs and activities did they become involved with? Well, the first thing we need to realize about the Early Church is that this was a people truly in love with God. The Holy Spirit was in charge of the church – not man. (Which is not to say that there weren't human leaders. There were men of great spiritual authority, anointed of God to lead the church. But they were constantly sensitive to the Holy Spirit in every decision they made). This was a GOD-LED church, not a man-led one. It was a church living in the midst of a great outpouring of the Holy Spirit. What a difference that makes!

Now, apart from gathering together in the open-air and from house to house, we find that the only real "program" the Jerusalem church seemed to have was one to feed the poor. They appointed seven 'deacons' (the word literally means "servants") who were "full of faith and of the Holy Spirit" – and they put them in charge of feeding and clothing the widows and orphans in a regular and systemized way. That was about it. This was their one real 'program'.

Now, I am not saying here that this is the only legitimate kind of program we can set up. But the point is, anything we decide to do must be DIRECTED BY THE HOLY SPIRIT – not yet another of man's "bright ideas". Also, I believe that, like 'Acts', most programs today should be aimed at reaching out to the poor and needy (Widows, prisoners, shut-ins, etc). This is clearly uppermost on God's heart. But even then, we need to be sensitive to His leading.

Some people have gone right over to the other extreme in this whole thing. They say that anything "organized" at all is completely wrong. That God will literally do everything that needs doing, and man should just 'wait' on Him to do it. Obviously, I cannot go along with this. It does not line up with the Book of Acts at all. God has always used HUMAN VESSELS to preach, teach, heal the sick, hold gatherings and prayer meetings, minister to the poor, etc. We see this in Acts. If it were ANGELS who were meant to be doing it, then they would. But God has given all of these tasks to us humans! And most of these things require at least some 'organizing'.

It is very clear that in Acts they did not wait for some "revelation from God" to tell them to meet together each day. They simply loved God and loved one another – so they gathered together in their homes every day – probably at a specific time. And it is obvious that there would probably have been a 'set time' when the apostles ministered in the open-air at Solomon's Porch as well. There is absolutely nothing to suggest that they would wait for some kind of 'angelic visitation' or a lightning-bolt from heaven before gathering together. It was simply the natural thing to do. And praying together and feeding the widows were natural things to do, as well. As I said, all of this involved some degree of "organization" (i.e., Arranging times and places, etc).

Many people take the concept of "resting in the Lord" too far. Are you someone who has truly learnt to REST in Him? Great! But does that now mean you do nothing at all? Of course not! Some people have grown spiritually lazy and are stuck in a rut – simply because they misunderstand "resting in the Lord". It is time to leave that 'rut' behind! Go and do all that God is telling you to do – but this time in the Spirit and not with fleshly striving like you used to! That is what 'resting' enables you to do. You can actually be very busy, as Jesus often was, yet still be "resting in the Lord".

The fear of 'organizing' or "leading" has actually been known to hinder or even destroy a number of Revivals in history. The Welsh Revival died after little more than ONE YEAR, when Evan Roberts (the man that God anointed and raised up to lead the Revival) actually HID HIMSELF AWAY because he did not want to lead any longer (he was convinced it would mean stealing glory from God). But really this was DISOBEDIENCE. Because God had raised him up to lead and he had a job to do. The most "humble" thing that we can do is simply WHATEVER God is telling us to do. If we are called to lead then it is a disaster for us to shrink back from it. Times of Revival are always times when leadership is at a premium and God searches the earth for those who are willing to pay the price and respond to His call.

A similar attitude to Evan Roberts prevailed in the Azusa Street meetings – where the leaders would hide themselves in prayer and allow ANYBODY to speak from the platform. Not just Christians but all kinds of charlatans and demonized characters sometimes were able to get up and preach, and this caused endless problems. A little authority sometimes goes a long way – and God rises up leaders for a REASON. There can be little doubt that the Azusa Revival faded away before its time – largely through failings like these.

It is a very delicate balance that leaders in Revivals face – how to keep everything on the rails without being too heavy-handed. How to give the Holy Spirit free reign – but not allow things to become so "loose" that the devil is able to wreak havoc as well. A difficult balancing act that requires great sensitivity to the Holy Spirit and a lot of wisdom. Many have tried and failed down the ages. But it is not impossible.

I think it is a very important fact that two of the most long-lived Revival movements in history were also the MOST ORGANIZED. They definitely involved powerful 'OUTPOURINGS' of the Holy Spirit, and yet there was a well-organized 'New Wineskin' that was formed to give the whole thing structure and long life. The moves of God that I am referring to here are the Wesleyan Revival (i.e., the Great Awakening in Britain) and the early Salvation Army. Both of these movements remained pretty much in a 'Revival' state for about 40 years apiece. Much longer than most Revivals by far.

What was the major key to this success? I believe it was the fact that both of these movements left behind the "old wineskin" and formed a totally new one – far closer to the Book of Acts. They did not try and cram the new move into the existing churches, but took the bold (and controversial) step of forming a truly NEW wineskin – leaving the old one behind. Interestingly, both of these movements were also "OUTDOORS"-based. They held great gatherings in the open air – out where the people were. They also had smaller meetings just for the converts. And they raised up "lay-preachers" (to the churches' great horror). They prayed without ceasing and preached fiery Revival sermons on repentance and the new birth. (The early Salvation Army modeled a lot of its preaching on Finney). These were some of the most glorious and long-lasting Revival movements in history. And not forgetting – they were also the MOST ORGANIZED.

So let us not fear leadership and organization, my friends! But let it always be by the leading of the Holy Spirit. It is man-made programs and the "good ideas" of men that we need to beware of. Somewhere there is a healthy balance in all of this. But I believe the only real balance can come when we are truly in a 'Revival' state. Then we will see the Holy Spirit truly take charge!

FURTHER BIBLE STUDY:

Ps 127:1, Lk 5:37, Acts 2:42-47, Acts 4:32-37, Acts 6:1-7.

CHAPTER FOURTEEN

WHAT ON EARTH IS "KOINONIA"?

The Greek word 'Koinonia' is the word that refers to the deep "fellowship" that the early Christians had together. It is something that many Christians today long for – and it really is the essence of 'church life' in the Bible. But to a very large degree the modern church seems to have lost it.

When we have a 'service' or meeting today, where everyone comes and sits in rows facing the front, sings some songs and listens to the sermon, then says "Bless you" to a few people and goes home – that is far from true 'koinonia'. Even in quite a few cell groups and house meetings today, there is little deep fellowship. It is more like a miniature "church service" – where a few people do all the 'ministry' and the rest sit around and watch.

We need to realize that 'koinonia' was at the very center of the way the early church lived out their lives. Without this, I do not believe that we truly have "church" at all. We may have a 'meeting' but we do not have deep fellowship. And without this, we really have nothing.

'Koinonia' relies on one thing above all others. It relies on a group of people coming together who truly are "washed-in-the-blood", Spirit-filled people. Because I believe that this kind of deep fellowship and joy and unity involves a "heart connection" on a real spiritual level – so the Holy Spirit can truly flow.

But the 'koinonia' of the early church involved other things, too. For one thing, it is clear that in their "house to house" meetings they gathered around a MEAL and also around the LORD'S SUPPER (more on this later). The early Christians partook of communion together EVERY DAY in their homes – that is how important it was to them.

Now, do you have to be a "special person" or an Elder to pray a blessing over communion and break bread with other believers in your home? Not at all. We are ALL "kings and priests". We should ALL be doing this kind of thing. We need to realize how important it is to break bread together with our families, our prayer groups, our house-fellowships and so-on. I don't believe we will ever get back to true New Testament 'koinonia' unless we do this.

The other thing they did in their house meetings (which were really their main 'fellowship' meetings) was that they gave room and encouraged EACH PERSON to move in the gifts of the Holy Spirit. This was not a "one man band" – far from it! Every single Spirit-filled believer was valued for who they were, and the giftings that they had. Read this very carefully: 1 Cor 14:26, "When you come together, EVERYONE has a hymn, or a word of instruction, a revelation, a tongue or an interpretation. All of these things MUST be done for the strengthening of the church" (NIV). (Remember, this kind of meeting is quite different from the large open-air meetings that the apostles held. What we are talking about here are the more intimate "home fellowships" that they had).

Notice too how different this is from the 'discussion' groups and Bible Studies that we often have today. This was a home meeting very deliberately aimed at seeing the Holy Spirit move and the members of the Body all ministering to one another in spiritual gifts. I believe we have to very consciously go down this path if we want to see this happen in our meetings. New believers need to be taught how to move in the gifts and there needs to be an environment where this is "normal". We need to choose whether we are just going to sit around 'discussing' things or whether we are going to invite the Holy Spirit to take charge.

Notice that Paul says 'EVERYONE' should be using their spiritual gifts in these meetings and that it is very important that ALL these giftings come forth. Spiritual songs, teaching, prophecies, tongues and interpretation – all these kinds of things. And I'm sure if there were sick or oppressed people present then there would be prayer for them also. This was a real "Holy Spirit" meeting, and to them it was "church as normal"!

It seems that these house-fellowships would have had 'elders' to guide things, and to step in if things got out of hand or if someone was bringing in deception. But I believe the role of an elder is more-or-less a "parenting" role. Keen to see God's children step out and flow in spiritual gifts and to grow up in the faith. I do not believe a true 'elder' would dominate such house meetings, but rather encourage others to come forward as much as possible. However, it certainly is his role to teach where necessary.

Imagine what it would be like if all our house-meetings were like this today. Imagine if we shared a "pot-luck" meal together, then partook of the Lord's Supper together – and then moved into a time where the members of the body all ministered to one another in spiritual gifts. While we are all in prayer, there might be tongues and interpretation or prophecies coming forth. There might be spiritual songs or words of knowledge. Someone might share a testimony or a prayer-need or a word of teaching.

What we are doing in such a setting is freeing the Holy Spirit to flow and move through us as He wills. And this is exactly what it was like to be part of the early church. So what are we waiting for??

DISTRACTIONS THAT HINDER

Earlier I made the point that deep 'koinonia'-type fellowship is usually very different from sitting around having a 'discussion'. Interestingly, someone who is involved in the "house-church" or 'Out-of-church' movement wrote a very telling email to me, describing how their meetings never seemed to enter into true 'koinonia': *"In our 'out-of-church' meetings this is not happening. It was actually happening more in some of our organized religious fellowship! Everyone spends so much time talking about the correct relational model of the church, correct doctrine, etc, that the spiritual gifts have been sidelined!!"*

Another couple wrote:

"When the Charismatic move first started in the late 60's, we were part of home meetings just like you described. They were great. Everyone shared as the Holy Spirit moved. Babies were allowed a bit of grace if they went on too long, and were gently and privately taken aside if they were in error or needed help. The meetings were in the Living Room and the Dining Room was off to the side – and moms and babies met there where the babies could crawl about and mamas could hear and give input if led by the Holy Spirit.

Bigger kids played in the bedroom of the host family with other kids or came and joined in the meetings. No kid was ever pushed off into "kids church". We believed that the anointing ministered to the kids regardless if they were coloring in books or sitting still taking it all in or just asleep on the floor...

We had tremendous meetings... How great things were - and should be again.

THE TRUTH ABOUT COMMUNION

A lot of us have been taught that Communion is largely a "symbolic" thing – or simply an act of 'remembrance'. But it is clear from the New Testament that the early Christians saw it as being much more than that. Otherwise, why would they have taken communion EVERY DAY from "house to house"? I mean, a symbolic ritual wouldn't be THAT urgent, would it? And also, if it was only 'symbolic', why did Paul say that a wrong attitude towards it was causing some of the Corinthian Christians to become weak and sick – and some even to DIE?? (1 Cor 11:29-30). I mean, how can a mere "symbol" have the power to actually make people that sick when it is misused?

The fact is, just like Baptism, the Lord's Supper is no "symbol" at all. It is a very real partaking of the "LIFE" of Jesus afresh. And it is very clear from all the New Testament writings on the subject that the apostles were very aware how powerful and important it was.

Now, we need to be careful not to go too far with this, because the Catholic Church has a very strange understanding of Communion. They believe that it actually becomes the real PHYSICAL FLESH and the real PHYSICAL BLOOD of Jesus. Which is kind-of surprising, when you think about it. Can you imagine eating real human flesh and drinking real human blood? No wonder the Protestants ran a mile in the opposite direction! However, based on the Scriptures it is obvious that what we are really partaking of in Communion is SPIRITUAL LIFE of the most potent kind – an actual refreshing within us of the "Bread of Life" and the cleansing "Blood of the New Covenant" that washes us from sin. We are supposed to partake of it by FAITH – a fresh impartation of the very essence of Jesus himself. You could even describe it as a kind-of refreshing of the "born again" experience, in a way.

Now all of this sounds pretty dramatic. But is there really proof for all of this in Scripture? Let's take a look:

Remember Jesus' words when he first partook of the Lord's Supper with his disciples: "Jesus took bread, gave thanks and broke it, and gave it to his disciples, saying, 'Take and eat; THIS IS MY BODY.' Then he took the cup, gave thanks and offered it to them, saying, 'Drink from it, all of you. THIS IS MY BLOOD of the covenant, which is poured out for many for the forgiveness of sins'" (Mt 26:26-28, NIV).

Notice that he did not say, "This is a SYMBOL of my body or blood." He said: "This IS my body, This IS my blood." And that is clearly the way his followers were to treat Communion from that time on. It was to be a REAL partaking of all the empowering and cleansing found in the spiritual body and blood of Jesus. It was to be taken in FAITH, receiving from God a fresh impartation each time.

Remember, Jesus had said these dramatic words: "I tell you the truth, unless you eat the flesh of the Son of Man and drink his blood, you have no life in you... For my flesh is real food and my blood is real drink" (John 6:53-55). In the same passage he had spoken of himself as the "bread of life" – the "bread that came down from heaven... He who feeds on this bread will live forever" (Jn 6:58).

Now we know that Jesus is also "the Word of God" as well as the 'bread of life'. This is the very essence of what we are partaking of here. And we know exactly what the 'blood' is all about too. All the way through Scripture we are told that "the LIFE is in the blood" and we are told that the blood of Jesus "cleanses us from all sin". My friends, are you ready to partake of Communion as a fresh impartation of these very things to you? If you are, then you are ready to partake if it just as they did in the Book of Acts. This is clearly why they partook of it every day. It was THAT important. They used Communion as a means of "abiding in Jesus" and partaking of his LIFE once more. It was like the Children of Israel who partook of the 'manna' in the wilderness each day to stay alive.

In modern times, I have heard of cases where people have actually been physically healed through partaking of communion in this deeper way. This is not surprising, because they are partaking of the very life and cleansing of Jesus by faith. We really need to be doing this all the time – just like the early church.

So what was it that the Corinthians were doing that actually seemed to turn the power of Communion against them? If you read the whole passage (1 Cor 11:17-34) you will see that the main problems seemed to be 1) Divisions amongst them, 2) Not "preferring" one another, and 3) Partaking of Communion in a very fleshly and carnal way.

Remember, communion is all about partaking of the "one body" of Christ. So it is not just 'oneness' with Jesus, it is also oneness with our brothers and sisters as well. It is a thing of true heart unity.

This is why Paul says, "A man ought to examine himself before he eats of the bread and drinks of the cup. For anyone who eats and drinks without recognizing the body of the Lord eats and drinks judgment upon himself" (1 Cor 11:28-29, NIV). So "heart unity" amongst the brethren is very important. If you have something against a brother or sister, it is important to go and make things right before taking communion.

To really get the most out of Communion, I believe it is important when praying a blessing over it to actually bless it publicly and openly as being the "body of Jesus" to us (the 'bread of life') and also the actual "blood of the New Covenant". To pray these things over Communion is important so that when people partake of it they can have FAITH that it will actually BE THAT to them. Then they are truly able to enter in.

Remember, we are ALL "kings and priests" therefore any one of us can pray and break bread amongst ourselves in our own homes and gatherings.

Some time ago in our home-meetings, we began the policy of sharing a meal and also communion together, and then moving into a time where everyone flows in spiritual gifts. I can see why this simple way of meeting worked so well in the early church. Sometimes in meetings like that you really feel like you could be in Acts. I am convinced more and more that the Holy Spirit wants to flow far more than He is allowed to in a lot of our meetings today. He is just waiting for the invitation.

Not long ago I read a wonderful little book about a Revival that occurred in Papua New Guinea during the late 1970's and on into the 1980's. Really, this Revival was based around all the things we have been discussing – the wonderful SIMPLICITY of New Testament Christianity. They learnt to do everything just as they saw it written in Acts.

It all started when some missionaries and nurses at a mission hospital repented deeply and were filled with the Holy Spirit. This movement soon spread outside the hospital and God challenged them to start living 'church life' as they saw it in the Bible. When somebody repented, instead of waiting for WEEKS or MONTHS afterward, they were baptized in the river STRAIGHT AWAY and prayed-for to receive the Holy Spirit. Healings started to occur. Demons were being cast out. They were led to cut down on 'sermons' and allow the members of the body to minister to one another in their meetings. The spiritual gifts began to flow amongst ALL believers, just like in the Bible. "Ordinary" Christians were encouraged to take communion in their homes and to baptize people. The whole thing simply exploded and spread from village to village! In a way it was a Revival "of the people". The 'everyday' believer being empowered to do the work of the kingdom.

And all they were doing were the 'SIMPLE' things. -\Just getting filled with the Holy Spirit and having 'koinonia'-type fellowship and doing the basic things found in the New Testament. Suddenly the Holy Spirit could flow. And thus, mighty REVIVAL came largely through practicing the kind of 'koinonia' concepts we have been talking about!

How simple this kind of thing is to start putting into practice, my friends. Let us not delay!

REPLIES FROM READERS:

Wendy W. wrote:

> *Our home fellowship is very small, just five adults and one child on a consistent basis, but the Lord has given us something very special: each of us would do anything to meet the needs of the others. We are deeply involved in each other's lives, both in prayer and in practical things. When one of us rejoices, we all rejoice, and if one of us struggles, we all struggle with him or her. We see each other as I understand Christians should see their brothers and sisters in the Lord – none of us is perfect, but all of us make room for each other's gifts and weaknesses. We*

all want the same thing: for the Lord to TRULY have His way in our lives. No games, and to borrow from Keith Green, no compromise. As often as is practical we eat together before we meet together, and everyone knows that our home and our table is always open to each of them and any guests they may want to bring, without notice, if they're hungry or need a place to stay. This is what I understand "normal" Christianity – the Christianity of the Bible – to be. It isn't rocket science, it's right there in the Book for everyone to read. Why do we insist on making it so difficult? Can we really call ourselves His children if we won't allow ourselves to be inconvenienced for each other? Was Jesus inconvenienced, just a little bit, for us?

<u>John E. wrote:</u>

I have been hungering for true body fellowship for a long time, and it doesn't seem to hardly even exist in the church anymore... I truly believe that we will have that glorious fellowship again when we repent of our worldly mindedness and determine to obey the Lord's commandment to (agape) love one another so much that we will begin again to gather in houses for daily communion, pot luck meals and fellowship, followed by Holy Spirit led times of body ministry and gifts as described in 1 Corinthians 14.

Can anyone deny that this is the biblical pattern that was given to us, or try to say that things are fine the way they are in the church, with no power, no true fellowship in the Biblical sense, and our love of one another waxed so cold that we only want to see each other once a week, if that often, and don't really want anyone to even know where we live?

CHAPTER FIFTEEN

LAST OF THE NINE - THE GOSPEL OF 'HUMANISM'

What is Humanism? It is all around us. It is the dominant spiritual creed of much of Western society today. It is rampant in the media, education, medicine – everywhere. And sadly it has infiltrated the church in a huge way in recent years. In Humanistic thinking, MAN is the center of all things rather than God. Everything revolves around making MAN happy. To talk about "SIN" makes people feel unhappy and guilty – therefore it is 'wrong' to be so "judgmental" as to preach strongly against sin. Humanism is very tolerant. "They are not hurting anybody," it says. "Let them do what they like." In fact 'TOLERANCE' and the 'HAPPINESS OF MAN' are the great mantras of Humanism.

So in what ways has this insidious philosophy invaded the church? Well, whenever you hear an evangelist sounding like a television commercial, then you are witnessing the invasion of Humanism. You will hear them say things like, "God wants to give YOU an exciting life. God wants to bless YOU. God wants to take away all your hurts and give you a happy life." Now of course there is truth in this. But what has happened here is that the EMPHASIS has shifted from "salvation from sin and judgment" to 'God wants to make you happy and blessed.' The focus is no longer on the fact that our sins offend a holy God, and that the CROSS is our only remedy. Rather, the message becomes more of a 'toothpaste commercial' – using Jesus as a means to have a happy and successful lifestyle. He becomes simply a means to our own selfish ends. It becomes all about "What can I get out of it?"

As the advertising industry has learned, there is a lot of money and success to be found in "eliminating the negative" and stressing only the positive and happy things. And a lot of preachers today seem to simply go along with this Humanistic tide – preaching mainly "blessings and grace" and forgetting about conviction of sin and 'taking up the cross'. For we wouldn't want to "offend" anybody, would we? But this is not what Jesus or the apostles were like. They preached 'sin, righteousness and judgment' in a very direct and piercing way. Often it is quite clear that their hearers were greatly offended – just as with the prophets of old. They preached real Repentance, 'counting the cost' and the loss of all things. But in many churches today that kind of talk would get you "never invited back". And thus the church becomes ripe for deception.

God is not primarily concerned with man's happiness. He is more concerned with our HOLINESS. But for many preachers, "Grace and Blessings" have become the recipes for success. And many are now treading that wide and seductive path. Quite a few of them have even learned how to raise their voice in such a way that you THINK they are preaching powerfully and challengingly. But when you actually examine what they are saying, it is usually more of the 'blessings and excitement' formula – simply ratcheted up a notch. And sadly, the church that feeds on such a "sugar and junk-food" diet will very quickly become utterly 'fat' and lukewarm.

The apostle Paul wrote: "For the time will come when men will not put up with sound doctrine. Instead, to suit their OWN DESIRES, they will gather around them a great number of teachers to say what their ITCHING EARS want to hear" (2 Tim 4:3, NIV). I have to say, there has never been a time in history that more blatantly fulfills this Scripture than today. We have literally PILES of "entertaining" teachers. We have never-ending conferences. We have every man and his dog on the "gravy train", tickling the Christians' ears and getting very well paid to do it. If you took away the ability to 'tickle ears', half the preachers (and prophets!) in America would be out of business overnight. They would have nothing left to say. They spend almost their WHOLE TIME preaching "agreeable" and exciting things to gullible Christians who will happily pay the registration fee, AND put money in the offering, AND put money in the 'second offering' AND THEN buy the set of tapes for some exorbitant fee. "Itching ears"? We have them by the truck-load today. Sadly, the old saying comes to remembrance: "Amusing ourselves to death." And thus, Humanism comes to dominate the church.

So what is God going to do about this state of affairs? Just what He has always done. He is going to find some hidden "nobodies" somewhere and He is going to put them at the back-side of the desert for just the right number of years, and He is going to train them up to be a company of 'John-the-Baptists' for such a time as this. And at the right moment they will come forth out of nowhere, speaking a piercing and uncompromising word: "Repent!" Such were the Finney's and Wesley's and Whitefields of centuries past. The history of Revival is the history of God's prophets coming forth at His divinely appointed time. Here is an incisive quote from A.W. Tozer which I have always loved:

"God has always had his specialists whose chief concern has been the moral breakdown, the decline in the spiritual health of the nation or the church. Such men were Elijah, Malachi and others of their kind who appeared at critical moments in history to reprove, rebuke and exhort in the name of God and righteousness.... Such a man was likely to be drastic, radical, possibly at times violent, and the curious crowd that gathered to watch him work soon branded him as extreme, fanatical, negative. And in a sense they were right. He was single-minded, severe, fearless, and these were the qualities the circumstances demanded. He shocked some, frightened others and alienated not a few, but he knew who had called him and what he was sent to do. His ministry was geared to the emergency, and that fact marked him out as different, a man apart." (From the Foreword to Ravenhill's 'Why Revival Tarries').

Humanism is in many ways the "unseen enemy" that is taking over the church today. It is a 'gospel of selfishness' that is infiltrating by subtlety and cunning. And the people love to have it so. They love men who can make them laugh, and avoid those who will make them weep. The dominant spiritual philosophy of the West is slowly becoming just as dominant in the church. Can men and women be found who will dare to "lift up a standard" against this ultra-POPULAR delusion – and preach the truth? Are there preachers who will dare to offend men if necessary, but their God never? The moment must come when such prophets will be found again. I pray that it is soon, because we are truly in an "emergency" today – as bad, or worse, than many that have gone before. Let the John-the-Baptists arise!

FURTHER BIBLE STUDY:

Jn 16:7-8, Heb 6:1-2, 2 Tim 4:2-4, Rom 2:16, Acts 17:30-31, Acts 24:24-25, 1 Cor 1:18-24, 1 Tim 4:1, Mt 13:22-23, 2 Th 2:9-11, 2 Cor 11:12-15.

CHAPTER SIXTEEN

WRAPPING IT ALL UP

The above series of articles provoked by far the largest response in the history of our Email List. There were literally thousands upon thousands of replies sent to me within just a few months; incredible, really.

So what was it that provoked all this comment? A lot of it was simply the desire to either strongly agree that "CHANGE" was needed on a large scale – or to defend the status-quo. Some even argued that the issues being discussed did not matter at all.

You mean it doesn't matter that the position of "pastor" today pretty much replicates the old Catholic "Priest" position – and is treated basically the same? It doesn't matter that this "Clergy/Laity" divide is still alive and well in the church?

And it doesn't matter that church buildings were never built by the early Christians at all? Many wrote to me and said I was making a mountain out of a molehill with this one. "The building is just a shell," they told me. But my point was that our buildings are also the CENTER-PIECE of the denominational DIVISIONS that we have today. And they also keep us hidden away from the very people we are called to reach.

Does it really matter that NO-ONE in the Bible ever became saved or 'born-again' by asking Jesus into their heart or 'repeating a little prayer'? Does it matter that ENFORCED 10% Giving (or "Tithing") was never preached to Christians, or that apostles and prophets ran the church rather than pastors? Does it matter that there were no Bible-colleges or theology degrees to help clever young men get trained "in their heads"? (Rather, the original leaders were uneducated fishermen and tax collectors who had been transformed in their HEARTS).

DOES ANY OF THIS MATTER AT ALL?

Does it matter that virtually nothing we do today was done like that in the original church? Our structures, our preaching, our priorities, our systems, our training, our GOSPEL – none of them seem to bear more than a passing resemblance to the Bible. In every way we are UTTERLY DIFFERENT from the church founded by Jesus and the apostles. When you take these issues one by one they may seem insignificant. But when you add them all up – can anyone tell me why we don't just call ourselves a DIFFERENT RELIGION and be done with it? I mean, we are virtually nothing like them, are we?

We talk a lot about "getting back to the book of Acts" today. But what if it involves removing all this junk? Who's going to take out the garbage? Is anybody really prepared to pay that kind of price? The rejection? The bitterness? The hatred?

Revival is one thing. "Reformation" is quite another. You can get killed with Reformation. Go ask Martin Luther.

One thing I am convinced of, there needs to be a large "ground-swell" of ordinary people desperate for 'CHANGE' for Reformation to succeed. And I don't think we see that yet. There is certainly the beginnings of it. But I don't think it is enough. To be honest, I think the only thing that can produce a groundswell of that magnitude would be another 'Great Awakening'. We need massive Revival to bring about the necessary desire for 'Reformation'.

However, I am truly convinced that Reformation must come with this Revival. For too long God has put up with our 'Dark Ages' structure. There must be a new wineskin, otherwise we will just find ourselves with another brief three-year Revival, like so many that have gone before. Old wineskins leak – that is the lesson of history. They cannot preserve a Revival. You cannot cram the 'new wine' into the old structures and expect it to last. As an historian I can tell you that the most long-lasting moves of God ALWAYS had a strong element of 'Reformation' about them. If a 'new wineskin' was created then sometimes the Revival was able to last for an entire generation. Glory to God! Can you imagine that?

As I stated near the beginning of this book, I am convinced that for the last 500 years, since the Great Reformation, God has used each wave of Revival to restore the church more and more to its original state. The first things He restored were 'justification by faith' and the 'priesthood of all believers'. Then in later moves of God we see the teaching of the 'new birth' and 'baptism by immersion' and 'holiness' being restored. Huge movements burst forth, evangelizing the earth and restoring lost Biblical truths. During this past century alone, the original "Baptism of the Holy Spirit" and all the gifts have finally been restored to the church. And since the 1960's virtually every Revival that has occurred around the world has been a full-on Holy Spirit-filled Revival, full of signs and miracles from God.

All the pieces are now in place for one last great push – a full return to the simplicity, the purity and the power of the early church. Despite all our advances, we have never seen an actual 'Book of Acts' church in all her raw beauty, holiness and power. Remember, Jesus is returning for a church that is "without spot or wrinkle or any such thing". I am praying that this coming Revival will see the end of the 'Reformation' process that has been ongoing now for 500 years. I pray that this will be the one that sees the final abandonment of all that is of 'Religion' – and a return to the pristine purity of the original.

When this process is complete, I believe that ONLY THEN can Jesus return for His beautiful Bride.

But all the timing is God's. And much preparation of HEART is needed, along with structural change. In fact, as I have always emphasized, it is the HEART issues that are the most important things.

As I said, all the pieces are now in place. Will you pray with me for one last great Revival and Reformation, my friends?

BRINGING BALANCE

I think it is very important at this point to try and bring some perspective to what we have been discussing, so that we don't get overly caught up in 'structural' matters, when it is the 'hearts' that should be our first concern.

When I was in my early twenties God took me to the 'school of hard knocks' for a little while and taught me a few basic lessons. The things I learned have stayed with me ever since.

At that time I had been doing a lot of Bible study and I probably had an understanding of about 70 percent of the "Nine Lies" material. But I was about to learn that 'theory' alone was not enough. Our outreach team at the time decided to start our own little fellowship – to "put the book of Acts into practice" as we thought. We were all Spirit-filled Christians, used to street evangelism. The fellowship we started held prayer meetings every morning, we had "plurality of elders", we baptized people in the sea and had communion and spiritual gifts operating (to a degree) in our meetings. We thought we were pretty cool. In fact, we thought we were "it".

We did everything we could to copy the book of Acts as we understood it. We had seen some success as an outreach team and we had every reason to assume that God would bless what we were doing now. After all, we were so "scriptural", right? We were so much like the Book of Acts, we thought – God was just BOUND to bless us.

And what was the result? Absolute abject failure. Nothing worked, nothing much happened, and our growth was virtually nil. I was shocked and devastated. What were we doing wrong? Couldn't God see how "scriptural" we were? Why on earth didn't He bless us?

Being young, it took me a while to come to grips with what the problems really were (quite a few years, in fact). These are the things God showed me: 1) We had an outward "form" of the book of Acts, but the "heart" was almost totally lacking; 2) We were more interested in getting things "technically" right and 'growing', rather than truly loving and caring for PEOPLE; 3) I had no true 'Revival' anointing, and without it a lot of my "Repentance" preaching was a waste of time; 4) I don't think we ever experienced true 'koinonia' at all in that group, even though we were doing many of the "technical" things right; 5) I was self-righteous and proud that we had so many things "correct", when in fact all the most vital things were missing. Personally, I realized later that I was a total 'Pharisee' – a proud religious zealot about "outward things" while the 'weightier matters' eluded me.

It took years of brokenness and 'crushing' for all these things to begin to be truly broken down in my life. It took years for me to start valuing PEOPLE more than technical correctness. It took years for me to see how much more important LOVE is than outward 'form'. And it took years for me to learn that it was the massive FLOWING of the Holy Spirit that made the early church what she was – NOT having all the "structural things right".

For years this crushing and brokenness was used by God to break down the self-righteous pride and 'religion' that I was steeped in. It was the very essence of 'wilderness'. And when I came out of that period I found that I was utterly changed.

These days I am under no illusions that we can simply do the "right things" and produce the Book of Acts. It is what we ARE, and not what we DO that is the crucial thing. I am under no illusions that simply applying all of the "9 Lies" and getting everything outwardly correct will do anything at all. If it is done at the right time, in the power of the Holy Spirit, then it can be very transforming. But otherwise it will achieve very little (if anything).

We need a Revival! We need the power of the Holy Spirit to sweep through. We need love and true 'koinonia'. We need a great 'Repentance' anointing on our preaching. Only then is it possible to see the Book of Acts happen again. And only then will changing our STRUCTURES on a large scale become truly worth doing.

This is why I often find I have a lot in common with some of my friends who do not share my convictions on the structure of the church. It is their 'heart' that matters to me. If these people are praying and longing for Revival, for instance, or loving and feeding the poor and preaching a powerful 'Repentance' message, or ministering powerfully in the Holy Spirit, then could it not be that they are over half-way to the Book of Acts already? For Acts was all about getting the "heart" things and the 'Holy Spirit' things right, far more than the structural 'forms'. Jesus did not go around preaching about the coming structure of the church. He preached repentance, love and the kingdom of God. He healed the sick and dealt with the heart issues – sin and pride. 'Structure' was not a priority at all.

To give you an example of what I am talking about, there is a Spirit-filled group in downtown Kansas City that has taken over an old run-down church building and they are feeding the poor and preaching repentance and caring for the unloved. Now, should I go bursting in there raving about "no church buildings in Acts", or should I bless what they are doing as being close to the 'heart' of true Christianity? I think I will take the latter course.

I find that I would much rather hang around with people who are deeply into prayer and intercession than people who spend all their time pondering how we can 're-structure' Christianity. I would rather sit down and talk to someone who truly preaches 'Repentance' than a person who thinks that we can change the church merely by emptying the people out of buildings and into houses. Friends, all that is doing is rearranging the 'boxes'. Unless there is massive 'heart' change to go with it then it is mostly a waste of time. I know because I have tried it – in several different configurations!

This is why "in-church", 'out-of-church' or "in-between" hardly matters to me. If I can see that on a 'heart' level a person is truly walking with God – praying and longing for Him to move by His Spirit, communing closely with Him and longing for transformation in the church – all of the other things pale into insignificance. I love meeting and fellowshipping with such people – wherever they are from. (And this includes pastors and other leaders. It is their 'heart' that matters).

When I look realistically at the "Nine Lies" issues, I see some that are of real use to us right now – and others that will only truly be useful AFTER a great move of the Holy Spirit has begun. It may be good to know about them now, but to see them actually come to pass will have to wait.

For instance, without a great move of God I cannot imagine the church suddenly deciding that it has no need of church buildings, professional clergy, Bible Colleges and the like. And even if these things were gotten rid of, THAT IN ITSELF would not change the heart of the church. We need Revival and THEN will come the Great Reformation and the new wineskin – when people can actually see the need for it. When the Holy Spirit has opened their eyes to see that structural change will help preserve the 'new wine' and make the church truly biblical. This is the order of events as I see it. Revival THEN Reformation. And thus, right now, anyone who is forging a path towards true Revival, repentance and heart-change in the church is a friend – no matter what their background.

Of course, as I said, there are other things from the "Nine Lies" series that can actually be of real value right now. For instance, the whole 'koinonia' thing can be wonderful – especially when meeting in homes. Coming together to eat and take communion and then seeing the Holy Spirit move as everyone (including children) flow in the gifts – this is a wonderful thing. (Part of this concept is the understanding that we can ALL baptize, we can ALL break bread in communion, and EVERYONE has giftings and a ministry from God). These 'koinonia' groups have the potential to truly transform lives. We have seen it.

Other aspects from the "9 Lies" series that we can enact right now include things like "united prayer", Repentance preaching, and the baptizing of new converts STRAIGHT AWAY – along with prayer for them to receive the Holy Spirit. And another thing that has come about through this series is that many people seem to have a renewed desire to STUDY THE BIBLE and find out for themselves what the early church was like. All of this is good.

But as for the larger aspects of it, I believe we will need massive REVIVAL before we can start to see some of those things come to pass. So keep on praying, my friends! Revival is truly the key.

DANGERS FOR THE "PURIST"

As I have experienced in my own life, it is quite possible to become overly "purist" about all the things we have been discussing. As I have said, God is not as concerned about outward 'form' as we often are. He will meet people wherever they are – whether it is in a Bible College or a church building or wherever. He is not "hung up" about such things. So while we look forward to a more "pure" church – far closer to Acts in every way – It is vital to remember that right now God will use ANYTHING and ANY PLACE to reach people by His Spirit. He does not confine Himself to only reaching out to people when they have "everything perfect" – and neither should we. The apostles preached in Synagogues and Greek Philosophy Schools and all kinds of places. They did not restrict God to moving only in "perfect" environments. God will move anywhere. And He may well call us into certain buildings for a season or into places where there is a particular group He wants us to reach. We need to be open to the Holy Spirit to do this kind of thing without being so "purist" that we actually miss the Lord.

Personally, I will go to any group or any building for any season that God desires me to do so, in order to minister to the people He is sending me to. One day perhaps He will cause a 'separation', and a stand will need to be made in these matters, but I do not see that occurring until large-scale Revival is well underway. In the meantime I am very happy to go anywhere and minister to whatever groups God is calling me to. And it is always the 'heart' things that I will major on when I minister there. For it is the 'heart' issues that are the keys to Revival, not the 'structural' things.

IN CONCLUSION

As we have seen, I believe we live in truly momentous days. I believe a great 'shaking' is coming to the church – a great tidal-wave of "CHANGE". And it is vital for us to understand what God wants to accomplish with this last great flood of Revival and Reformation. He wants a pure and holy bride for His Son. He wants a last-days Church that shines His glory like a beacon into the world – before tribulation and darkness cover the landscape in her final hours.

There is a new church coming. Are you ready? There is a call going out for leaders who welcome 'change' – who do not resist the Holy Spirit – who are desperate to see the church transformed. Could you be one of these?

The hour is late and God's eyes roam the earth to find those who will "stand in the gap" before Him for the land. To find praying people who give Him no rest day or night, but who cry out with an agonized heart that the glory of the Lord be established in the earth once more – so that all men may repent. I pray that you and I may be found in this number, my friends. God bless you all.

VISIT OUR WEBSITE-

www.revivalschool.com